Where to SURREY

THE INFORMATIVE GUIDE TO EATING OUT IN SURREY

Editor: Jeff Evans
Art and Design: Lyndsey Blackburn, Sue Morgan
Editorial Assistant: Jackie Horne
Compilation: Gail Ellison

CONTENTS

Cover Photograph: The Onslow Arms Inn, West Clandon

Published by Kingsclere Publications Ltd.
Highfield House, 2 Highfield Avenue,
Newbury, Berkshire, RG14 5DS

Typeset by Wessex Press of Warminster Limited, Wiltshire
Produced through MRM Associates, Reading, Berkshire

Distributed in the UK by AA Publishing,
The Automobile Association,
Fanum House, Basingstoke, Hampshire, RG21 2EA

Extreme care is taken to ensure the accuracy of entries, but
neither the Editor nor the Publishers accept any liability
for errors, omissions or other mistakes, or any
consequences arising therefrom.

ISBN 0 86204 136 8

Foreword

Ian Hayton

BY IAN HAYTON

I came to live in Surrey 24 years ago. Then, as now, it was a beautiful county, full of charm, but, as far as eating out was concerned, a veritable wasteland. If a guide had been published then it would have been a very slim volume indeed.

Fortunately, time cures most ailments and, today, the variety and choice is impressive, ranging from haute cuisine to simple bistro fare and covering culinary delights from all points of the compass. Design and comfort have developed to a fine degree; long gone are the flock wallpaper and hard chairs of the 60's. Atmosphere and service are as important now as the dishes placed before us.

The hospitality industry has grown considerably and is now leading the country in job creation (over 1,000 jobs per week). We are eating out more, on average 25 times a year, and the people attracted to make a career in the industry are young, enthusiastic and very creative.

Where to Eat helps you make your choice; visit one or all, but enjoy — that is what the industry is there for.

Ian A Hayton,
Managing Director,
Foxhills, Ottershaw.

Tastes of SURREY

Surrey is a county which has been taken much for granted. Its proximity to London has meant that most visitors to the area have been merely passing through, a situation even more true today in this age of high-speed trains, impersonal motorways and fast jets. It has also had the image of being London's back garden, shipping out much of its produce to the capital to feed its vast population, with the very best, of course, saved for royalty and nobility. As a result, whilst its hospitality trade has flourished through centuries of providing refreshment to coach travellers or those using the waterways, its wealth of good food and drink has been little extolled and the use of its quality produce seldom encouraged outside the royal households. Its best cooks found employ in the city and perhaps took with them the inspiration to create enduring recipes and culinary treats such as are seen in other parts of Britain.

Even in the earliest days Surrey's rural prosperity was noted. The records show extensive sheep farming throughout the county. Market gardening was widespread in the west and the wooded hills always a source of wealth for the hunter. Royalty indulged itself in the chases which teemed with wildlife, and the 'gourmet' king himself, Henry VIII, took considerable pleasure in what provided him with both sport and supper. Indeed, with Surrey studded with palaces, kings and queens over the years have had a major influence on Surrey's culinary development. Only the best, of course, found its way to the royal table — but the county could happily provide. Venison and

pheasant from the royal parks, swans from the Thames and game birds and fish of all kinds filled palace larders time and again.

Surrey chickens were the Aylesbury ducks of their day. Specially fattened on milk-soaked corn and

raisins, and housed in coops which were illuminated at night so that feeding could continue, they were always associated with noble feasts. An early Guildford recipe serves them cooked with peaches and another local preparation sees chicken disguised as a lizard, echoing bizarre Roman methods of disguising delicious food as the most revolting animal. The fun here was in discerning that beneath the 'scales' which were made of tiny coloured omelettes there was succulent, richly-stuffed chicken and not some unappetising reptile.

When good King Henry took possession of beautiful Hampton Court from Cardinal Wolsey, he soon ordered the construction of a second kitchen, as the original was not up to the task of catering for the royal needs. Thoughts immediately come to mind of Charles Laughton slinging chicken bones over his shoulder and spluttering his way, mouth-full, through a gargantuan feast. Such gluttony may well be a caricature but revelry, indeed, was not stinted. Feasts often saw up to 3,000 guests in attendance.

Along the river, chicken again found its use in a dish known as Richmond Froise. Served as an accompaniment at many a banquet, it was a kind of filled pancake where the filling — in this case chicken, bacon and cubes of fried bread — was added to the batter rather than being folded in during cooking. Fish, too, was a favourite and the rivers of Surrey

still run well with coarse fish. The Thames, of course, needs no introduction, but the Mole, too, is rich in dace, chubb and roach, and the Wey filled with bream, grayling and roach. The canals, too, provide anglers with much scope.

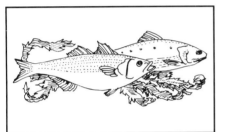

Away from the banks, local fruit and vegetables have always flourished. 'Pick your own' farms not only offer a bargain but provide a thoroughly enjoyable summer's day out. Soft fruits are favourites,

worms feeding off the leaves, failed on account of the climate, the sticky, easily ripened fruits were often combined with apples and made into tarts. Vegetable-wise look no further than the humble pea, celebrated for centuries in recipes like Weybridge's Peas in Cream, with the addition of mint, parsley, spring onions and sugar.

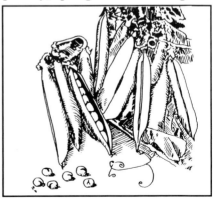

though it is unlikely that you will be able to find mulberries, particularly popular in Tudor and Stuart times. Although attempts to establish a silk industry, with the

Fruits of the vine, too, have growing importance in this part of the South East. Although Surrey is not as favoured as neighbouring Sussex or Kent in this capacity, wine making is, all the same, a developing industry, with benefits for tourism too. Visit the Hascombe Vineyard, near Godalming, for example, and indulge yourself in a tour and tasting. There are numerous farm visits too. Loseley Farm at Guildford

is famous for its herd of Jersey cows which produce the finest creams, yoghurts and ice cream. Indeed, it is significant that the Milk Marketing Board has its head-quarters in the county. So, too, does the Brewing Industry Foundation, which is rather ironic in view of the fact that Surrey no longer brews much beer. Friary Meux is one of the predominant brewers in the county, with some 600 pubs in the South East. The original brewery in Guildford closed in 1969 but its popular beers are still brewed in other plants in Burton-on-Trent and Romford.

Today, of course, Surrey is a gourmet's dream; one can eat Continentally or internationally; formally or informally, and in the nouvelle or classique styles. It is a shame that, for a county with so much to offer the chef, traditional Surrey cooking is more difficult to come by. One may, of course, be able to discover some of the recipes already mentioned, or even indulge oneself on a royal favourite like

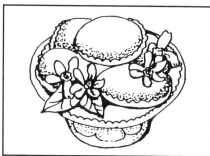

Maids of Honour cakes, to which Henry VIII was known to be partial. And one other titbit to offer, should Surrey ever be accused of being totally bereft of culinary flair, is that Mrs Beeton herself was brought up living in the grandstand of Epsom racecourse! She clearly did not take Surrey for granted.

Chef's Choice

In each of our regional **Where to Eat** *guides, we ask an experienced chef, well-respected in the area, to provide one of his favourite menus:*

Jean-Yves Morel, born near Lyons, is one of Britain's foremost chefs. He trained as a charcutier before arriving in England and taking up a position with the Roux brothers at Le Gavroche, London. After working for several years in other top London establishments, he and his wife, Mary-Anne, opened their own restaurant in a 300-year-old cottage in Haslemere, in July 1980.

Jean-Yves and Mary-Anne Morel

His philosophy is based on fresh ingredients and quality rather than quantity and the years which have followed have seen accolade after accolade bestowed on Morels. These include a Michelin star and the award of Egon Ronay Restaurant of the Year 1988. Here Jean-Yves reveals a selection of his favourite dishes.

AMUSE GUEULE
Gruyère and Parmesan Soufflé
*A tantaliser to whet the appetite,
served with an aperitif.*

STARTER

Blini

WINE
**Pouilly-Fumé 'Cuvée Prestige'
1985**

*A Russian pancake with smoked
salmon, caviar and sour cream,
accompanied by a dry white wine,
with a slightly smoky taste to
complement the smoked salmon.*

SORBET
To freshen the palate.

FISH COURSE
Nage de Poissons et Crustacés

WINE
**Rully Blanc ler Cru, J Drury
1986**
*A mixture of Dover sole,
salmon, turbot, langoustine
and scallops, served with a
vegetable and white wine*

*liquor scented with
coriander and star annis. A
dry and fruity wine from the
Côte Chalonaise.*

MAIN COURSE
**Filet d'Agneau et sa Panouffle
au Basilic, son Jus**

WINE
Fleurie, André Collange 1987
*Fillet of English lamb topped with a
basil mousseline and served with the
pan juice, accompanied by a light
and fruity red from south Burgundy.
A spring dish: "flavours which
remind one of the early spring sun".*

DESSERT
Creme Grandmère

WINE
**Muscat de Beaumes de Venise
'Domaine de Coyeux', Yves
Nativelle 1985**
*This version of crème
brûlée, served with
fresh fruit and
home-made sorbet, is
a light dessert to
complete the meal.*

COFFEE AND PETITS FOURS

Introduction

This *Where to Eat* guide has been compiled to offer readers a good cross-section of eating places in the area. We do not only concentrate on the most expensive or the 'most highly rated' but endeavour to provide details of establishments which cater for all tastes, styles, budgets and occasions. Readers may discover restaurants (formal and informal), pubs, wine bars, coffee shops and tearooms and we thank proprietors and managers for providing the factual information.

We do not intend to compete with the established 'gourmet guides'. *Where to Eat* gives the facts — opening hours and average prices — combined with a brief description of the establishment. We do not use symbols or ratings. *Where to Eat* simply sets the scene and allows you to make the choice.

We state whether an establishment is open for lunch or dinner and prices quoted are for an à la carte three course meal or a table d'hôte menu, including service, as well as an indication of the lowest priced wine. However, whilst we believe these details are correct, it is suggested that readers check, when making a reservation, that prices and other facts quoted meet their requirements.

Two indexes are included at the back of the guide so that readers can easily pinpoint an establishment or a town or village. We always advise readers to use these indexes as, occasionally, late changes can result in establishments not appearing in a strictly logical sequence.

We hope that *Where to Eat* will provide you with the basis for many intimate dinners, special family occasions, successful business lunches or, perhaps, just an informal snack. A mention of this guide when you book may prove worthwhile. Let us know how things turned out. We are always pleased to hear from readers, be it praise, recommendations or criticism. Mark your envelopes for the attention of 'The Editor, Where to Eat Series'. Our address is:

Kingsclere Publications Ltd.
Highfield House, 2 Highfield Avenue,
Newbury, Berkshire. RG14 5DS.

We look forward to hearing from you. Don't forget, *Where to Eat* guides are now available for nearly every region of Britain, Ireland and the Channel Islands, each freshly researched and revised every year. If you're planning a holiday contact us for the relevant guide. Details are to be found within this book.

Where to Eat
SURREY

LEMONGRASS GOURMET THAI RESTAURANT

54 Fife Road, Kingston-upon-Thames.
Tel: (01) 546 8221

Hours: *Open for lunch and dinner (last orders 10.30pm).*
Average Prices: A la Carte £18; set menu from £12; lunch special £4.50.
Wines: *House wine £6.60 per bottle.*

Lemongrass is a Thai herb with a tangy lemon fragrance — an apt name for a restaurant offering the finest traditions of Thai cuisine. The décor similarly echoes the name, its creams and yellow creating a restful atmosphere. Thai cooking, which can be spicy and hot, is exemplified in such starters as the traditional tom yum soup, based on chicken broth with lemongrass, lime and chillies and served in variations such as tom yum goong (with added prawns and straw mushrooms). For a main course dish there are some yum salads, again a traditional method using fresh herbs, lemon juice and chillies, which results in a particularly spicy salad, and dishes like yum plameuk (including slices of squid and red onions). Other popular dishes are gang keowan gai (hot Thai curry with chicken, bamboo shoots, green chillies and coconut milk) and pud khing (stir-fried meat with fresh ginger, special black mushrooms and spicy onions). To finish off there are refreshing desserts such as itim ma proa (coconut and pineapple ice cream served in a whole baby coconut). A take away service is also available. Situated near Bentalls.

THAI FOOD

*Come and experience
the very best is
Gourmet Thai Cuisine*

54 FIFE ROAD, KINGSTON UPON THAMES
TELEPHONE: 01-546 8221

CHEZ MAX

85 Maple Road, Surbiton. Tel: (01) 399 2365

Hours: *Open for lunch and dinner (last orders 10pm).*
Closed Sat lunch/Sun/Mon.

Average Prices: *A la Carte £21; Table d'Hôte £16.50.*

Wines: *House wine £8.50 per bottle.*

Chef-proprietor Max Markarian has an impeccable culinary pedigree. Having trained at Le Caprice and worked with Prue Leith on various TV programmes, he has now been running his own restaurant for six years and has established a loyal following for his generously proportioned nouvelle cuisine. Crudités are provided for each table, whilst the menu itself offers about six dishes per course. Begin with oeuf en timbale au fromage et aux épinards (cheese mousse with a spinach and cream sauce), or salmon cru aux concombres et aux épinards (marinated salmon with cucumber on a bed of spinach). For a main course dish there are aiguillettes de canard, vinaigrette de framboises (breast of duck with a sweet and sour raspberry sauce), foie de veau aux raisins (Dutch calves' liver with a grape sauce), and suprême de pintade aux échalotes (breast of guinea fowl with roast garlic and shallots). To conclude try some of the truffle cake with orange and Grand Marnier, or the delicate tulip of almond tiles stuffed with fresh fruits. Alternatively, there is Stilton and walnut pâté with a port jelly.

Chez Max. Tel: 01 399 2365

13

CARS CAFE (RESTAURANT BAR)

7–9 Brighton Road, Surbiton.
Tel: (01) 399 1582

Hours: Open for coffee, lunch, tea and dinner (last orders 11.30pm).

Average Prices: A la Carte £8; Sun lunch £5.95; snacks from £1.45.

Wines: House wine £5.25 per bottle.

The success of Cars Café is derived from its combination of an interesting and fun backdrop with 'Tex-Mex' cooking. Motoring memorabilia is everywhere; there's a Morris 1000, a Mustang and even the odd petrol pump in attendance. The menu itself ranges over American-style hamburgers, Mexican dishes and specialities such as chicken breast with garlic butter and rice. For a taste of Mexico try corn taco shells with guacamole, bean dip and chilli-con-carne, or quesadillas (grated cheese and onion in a flour tortilla with rice and a spicy red bean sauce). To conclude there are favourites such as cheesecake, crumbles and apple pie, plus some very appetising ice cream concoctions. These include 'antifreeze' for two people (vanilla and maple/walnut ice cream with honey, sultanas, nuts, brandy, pineapple, fresh cream and toasted almonds). 60's and 70's music buffs will be in their element on Monday nights, whilst the summer months see al fresco dining. There is also a private party room upstairs.

Cars Cafe

Mexican and American food
and Cocktails
Served in an informal
and lively atmosphere

7–9 Brighton Road, Surbiton. Telephone: 01-399 1582

BOMBAY PALACE RESTAURANT

15–17 Hill Rise, Richmond.
Tel: (01) 940 3002/948 4983

Hours: *Open for lunch and dinner (last orders 11.15pm).*
Average Prices: *A la Carte £12.*
Wines: *House wine £6.50 per bottle.*

The prestigious chain of the Bombay Palace has become internationally well-known for its export of the finest traditions of Indian cuisine. The décor of the Richmond restaurant is elegant with crisp pink table linen offset by an assortment of potted plants and colourful old prints along the walls. The menu itself is divided into seven sections with seafood, chicken, lamb, vegetable, rice and chef's specialities, enhanced by the addition of some tandoori dishes. The choice includes dishes such as chicken karahi (diced chicken cooked in spices, tomatoes, ginger and green chillis, served sizzling in an iron souk-karahi), mattar paneer (home-made cheese and green peas cooked with onion, tomatoes, yoghurt and Indian spices), and lamb biriani (special Basmati rice cooked with tender pieces of lamb, garnished with almonds and nuts and served with a separate curry sauce). There are also special set Palace dinners and a vegetable thali. On Sundays a buffet is available which is always popular with family parties. Large cocktail bar for pre-dinner drinks.

THE CASTLE

21 Thames Street, Sunbury-on-Thames.
Tel: (0932) 783647

Hours: *Open for lunch and dinner (last orders 10pm).*
Closed Sat lunch/Sun.

Average Prices: Set menu £15.70. House wine £7.50 per bottle.

A listed 17th century building, The Castle is imbued with an authentic and tastefully preserved period atmosphere. Gilt framed oils and 18th century furnishings combine with a backdrop of dark green to recreate the stylish elegance of the Georgian era. It is a lovely setting in which to enjoy the French classic and regional dishes of patron Giuseppe. Dishes are seasonally based, with game a feature of the winter months and all ingredients brought fresh from the markets daily. Fish from Billingsgate, prime Scotch Angus beef, Dutch veal and English and Welsh lamb are all enriched by a skilful use of sauces. Examples of the culinary flair can be seen in starters such as king prawns, frog's legs and crab sautéd in garlic butter, white wine and herbs, followed by main course dishes like tournedo St Genevieve (Scotch fillet filled with pâté, flambéd in brandy and served with Madeira, mushrooms, ham and a cream sauce). For dessert there is a rich chocolate mousse laced with rum and sultanas. Wines are predominantly French, carefully chosen and modestly priced. Ideal venue for many functions.

THE RUNNYMEDE HOTEL

	Windsor Road, Egham. Tel: (0784) 436171
Hours:	*Open for coffee, lunch, tea and dinner (last orders 9.45pm, 10pm Sat, 9.30pm Sun).*
Average Prices:	*A la Carte £27; Table d'Hôte £14.75.*
Wines:	*House wine £8.75 per bottle.*

The Runnymede Hotel is an airy, modern hotel situated on the banks of the Thames, where clients are welcomed with old-fashioned courtesy and a totally new look in décor and ambience. At lunchtime diners can relax and enjoy the ever-changing Thames-side view, whilst in the evenings the gardens and river are floodlit to provide a romantic setting for dinner. The style is classical, with a number of low-calorie dishes featured on the à la carte selection. Begin with saumon fumé poché (smoked salmon, poached and served on a chive butter sauce with salmon caviar), to be followed by dishes such as escalopes de veau au Marsala (veal in a sauce of Marsala and cream), or cailles farcies aux raisins (quail stuffed with grapes). For dessert try soufflé glacé mange-tout (iced Grand Marnier soufflé served in a chocolate cup), followed by coffee and home-made petits fours. Exquisite presentation on Limoges porcelain is an added pleasure. The Saturday night dinner dance and the traditional Sunday luncheon continue to grow in popularity, with booking now essential for both.

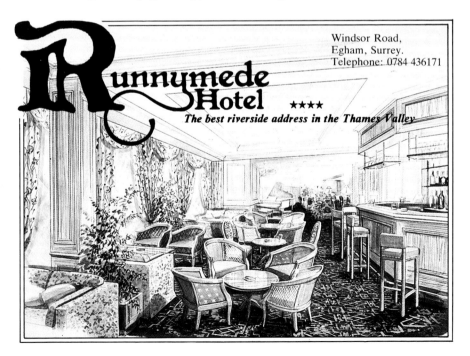

Runnymede Hotel ★★★★
The best riverside address in the Thames Valley

Windsor Road, Egham, Surrey.
Telephone: 0784 436171

ANGELO'S

70 Terrace Road, Walton-on-Thames.
Tel: (0932) 241964

Hours:	*Open for lunch and dinner (last orders 10pm).*
	Closed Sunday.
Average Prices:	*A la Carte £13; Table d'Hôte £12.*
Wines:	*House wine £6 per bottle.*

For the last 19 years Angelo's has been well-known for the warm welcoming ways of Angelo and Ivana Minerva, who run their restaurant like an Italian family home. Their Italian cucina, and in particular the patron's flair with seafood, has built them a solid local following. The best produce is professionally prepared and attractively presented, and, whilst Angelo admits to seafood being his first love, his home-made pastas and risottos are also particularly popular and make appetising starters. The main course covers fish, meat and poultry dishes, all authentically prepared, whilst there are some appetising desserts to round off the meal: one selection involves soaking in brandy marinade for several days. The wine list is, not surprisingly, Italy orientated, with Tuscan labels to the fore. There is also a table d'hôte menu which changes seasonally to secure the best of the market's produce. Reservations are recommended, particularly for the weekend.

Angelo's

FOR THE BEST ITALIAN CUCINA

Angelo's is a restaurant for your special occasion. We are renowned for our extensive choice of Italian Speciality dishes.

Tel: WALTON
(0932) 241964

70 TERRACE ROAD
WALTON
SURREY

THE COLONY RESTAURANT

3 Balfour Road, Weybridge.
Tel: (0932) 842766/855544

Hours: *Open for lunch and dinner (last orders 11pm).*
Average Prices: *A la Carte £17–£20.*
Wines: *House wine £6.50 per bottle.*

The Colony has established a strong local reputation since it opened four years ago. As Chinese cookery is based on a contrast of tastes, so here the restaurant décor contrasts colour. White walls are set against black beaming, with numerous potted plants and a weeping fig tree adding to the overall atmosphere. The cuisine is Pekinese and the presentation delicate, revealing the chef's artistry. For an unusual starter try squab (finely chopped prawn and pork wrapped in iceberg lettuce), toasted prawns with sesame seeds, or fried won-ton (crispy fried pastry served with a sweet and sour sauce). For a main course dish there is scampi Peking (stripped scampi served with ginger and garlic after deep-frying), Konchin king prawns (stir-fried with ginger, garlic and a sauce), sizzled beefsteak with black bean and chilli, and diced chicken and cashew nut in a yellow bean sauce. For dessert try the traditional toffee banana or some lychees. There is also a modest wine list where the range all the same takes in champagne and saké. Weekend reservations helpful.

THE SHIP THISTLE HOTEL

Monument Green, Weybridge.
Tel: (0932) 848364

Hours: *Open for morning coffee, lunch (except Sat), afternoon tea and dinner (last orders 10pm, 9.30pm Sun).*

Average Prices: *A la Carte £18.50; set dinner menu £13.75; lunch £9.75.*

Wines: *House wine £7.50 per bottle.*

L'Escales Restaurant at The Ship has a warm and homely atmosphere with white table linen setting off the dark mahogany of the panelling and co-ordinated furnishings. The restaurant is small and intimate and bookings are advised for most evenings. Chef is Peter Charlton who has developed his menu over 13 years here and whose book on fish preparation and cookery is recommended reading in training colleges. Try his symphony of seafood or his baked sea bass in a herb crust, or, if your preference is not for fish, there is a wide variety of dishes to suit all tastes. These include smoked chicken breast with beanshoots, medallions of veal, lamb and beef, served on a trio of sauces, and loin of lamb baked with thyme and spinach. Flambés are available and there are noted cheese and dessert selections from the trolley to conclude. Vegetarians are catered for and live music from a sole guitarist is an added attraction on Saturday evenings.

THE BROADWATER RESTAURANT AT OATLANDS PARK HOTEL

Oatlands Drive, Weybridge. Tel: (0932) 847242

Hours: *Open for coffee, lunch, tea and dinner (last orders 10pm). Closed Sat lunch.*

Average Prices: *A la Carte £22; Sun lunch £12.95; snacks from £1.95.*

Wines: *House wine £7.95 per bottle.*

Oatlands Park Hotel has recently undergone a £4.2 million refurbishment which has mostly restored it to its former Victorian splendour. Particularly striking is the glass domed lounge where afternoon tea is served in elegant comfort. The high-ceilinged restaurant is at its liveliest at Sunday lunchtime when a jazz trio is playing, but during the rest of the week a resident pianist plays soothingly in the background. The menu itself is Anglo-French and with unusual starters such as Cullen Skink (a delicately flavoured fish broth made with smoked finnan haddock, potatoes, onions and milk). Its name comes from Cullen, the Moray Firth fishing village, and skink, an old Scots name for broth. The main course has an oriental flavour with its Indonesian nasi goreng and Thai prawn curry, but there are also more traditional dishes such as fillet of beef lyonnaise (served on a bread croûton with a sauce of lyonnaise onions, topped with breadcrumbs, truffle and grated Parmesan) and breast of duck with a pink peppercorn sauce. Desserts are flambéd.

The BROADWATER *Restaurant*

Oatlands Park Hotel, Oatlands Drive, Weybridge
Tel: (0932) 847242

CAMERON'S RESTAURANT

131 Oatlands Drive, Oatlands Village, Weybridge.
Tel: (0932) 843604
Hours: *Open for lunch and dinner. Closed Sat lunch/Sun.*
Average Prices: A la Carte £14.95; wine £5.95 per bottle.

Jennifer Cameron has been running her own restaurant since 1986 and offers an Anglo-French menu that changes weekly. Begin with mussels with ginger and chilli, followed by strips of calves' liver with a lime butter sauce, or veal escalopes with a wild mushroom and Madeira sauce. Carob and orange roulade might conclude, and there is a selection of popular and mainly French wines to accompany.

cameron's
restaurant

131 Oatlands Drive,
Oatlands Village,
Weybridge,
Surrey.
Tel: (0932) 843604

VECCHIA ROMA

55–57 Bridge Road, East Molesey. Tel: (01) 979 5490
Hours: *Open for lunch and dinner (last orders 11pm).*
Closed Sat lunch.
Average Prices: A la Carte £20; Table d'Hôte £13.50; wine £6.50.

"When in Rome", as the saying goes, or even when in East Molesey, as here the Italian spirit is recaptured by proprietor Toni Di Michele. Traditionally cooked Italian dishes include piccatine di vitello alla melanzana (veal with aubergines), and agnello contadina (lamb). There are seasonal daily specials and parties large or small are easily catered for. The wine list has both Italian and other Continental choices.

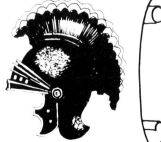

Toni Dimichele Welcomes You To the

VECCHIA ROMA

For the very best in Italian Cuisine
55/57 Bridge Road, East Molesey, Surrey
Telephone 01 - 979 - 5490
and 01 - 941 - 5337

BASTIANS

Hampton Court Road, East Molesey.
Tel: (01) 977 6074

Hours: Open for lunch and dinner (last orders 10.30pm).
Closed Sat lunch/Sun.

Average Prices: A la Carte £18.

Wines: House wine £6.95 per bottle.

Bastians, situated opposite the maze at Hampton Court, is perhaps the restaurant that Henry VIII would have brought the odd pretty thing to had it been open in his day. On entering, the first thing that diners usually notice is the apple wood log fire blazing away, with other diners sipping pre-dinner cocktails and browsing through the menu. The atmosphere is further enhanced by the furnishings and interesting artefacts. The tables are well spaced so that it is possible to talk sweet nothings or big business in complete privacy. Chef Eric Armitage has cleverly translated some traditional French dishes into his own inimitable style, offering specialities such as crab and papaya, fillet Dijon, prawns in garlic and lemon butter, and a salad de patron (with artichoke leaves, fresh figs, fennel, pomegranate seeds, walnuts, lettuce and a hint of walnut oil in the dressing). On the pudding menu there is crème brûlée made to Henry VIII's own recipe.

BASTIANS
RESTAURANT
Tel:
01-977 6074

CAMEMBERT
RESTAURANT
Tel:
01-977 0869

THE CAMEMBERT RESTAURANT

Hampton Court Road, East Molesey. Tel: (01) 977 0869

Hours: Open for dinner (last orders 10.30pm). Closed
Fri/Sat evenings.

Average Prices: A la Carte £15; wine £6.95 per bottle.

The Camembert Restaurant is situated on the first floor, above its sister establishment Bastians Restaurant. Its informal atmosphere is partnered by value for money dishes from a Continental menu. Try the traditionally-English salt beef with dumplings, one of the pasta dishes, or the restaurant's famous Camembert frite with a tangy home-made gooseberry sauce.

MEDICI

7 Station Approach, Hinchley Wood.
Tel: (01) 398 9952/9953

Hours: *Open for lunch and dinner (last orders 10pm).*
                    Closed Sat lunch/Sun evening/Mon.
Average Prices: *A la Carte £14.50; Sun lunch £10.50.*
Wines: *House wine £6.50 per bottle.*

The name Medici recalls the famous and powerful Renaissance Florentine family, many of whose portraits line the walls of this restaurant which is decorated to an art deco style of contrasting grey, black and white. The menu is international, but predominantly Italian, and agreeably priced. Try the antipasto misto (mixed hors d'oeuvre) for a starter, or trio di paste, a combination of three different pasta dishes. The main course covers a selection of seasonal fish and meat dishes with popular favourites such as chicken Mediterraneo (breast of chicken topped with prawns and served with a white wine, garlic and cream sauce). A sweet trolley concludes, supplemented by temptations such as crème brûlée or Floating Islands (soft meringues served with a caramel and vanilla sauce). The wine list is modest, but the selection ample. Vegetarians will also find dishes to please and there is a Sunday three course lunch offering a traditional roast and Italian dishes. Private parties accommodated. Visa and Access cards are accepted.

MEDICI RESTAURANT

FOR THE BEST IN
INTERNATIONAL
CUISINE

7 STATION APPROACH
HINCHLEY WOOD

RESERVATIONS:
TEL: 01-398 9952/3

LES ALOUETTES

7 High Street, Claygate.
Tel: (0372) 64882

Hours: *Open for lunch and dinner (last orders 10pm).*
Closed Sat lunch/Sun.

Average Prices: *A la Carte lunch £18; dinner £23.*

Wines: *House wine £8.50 per bottle.*

Les Alouettes' atmosphere is relaxed and the service unhurried. Great care and thought has been put into all aspects of the restaurant, right down to the smallest detail. The décor is one of soft grey and is balanced by the crisp white napery, sparkling crystal and fresh flowers which grace the tables. The menu itself is composed of dishes cooked to a modern French style and with many of the ingredients imported direct from France. Chef Michel Perraud is responsible for dishes such as tournedos poêle aux pleurottes et à la bordelaise (Scotch fillet of beef with oyster mushrooms, glazed shallots and a rich wine sauce). Business lunches are a further attraction. The modest price does not preclude quality dishes and they are served in an atmosphere and setting conducive to ensuring the success of an impressionable executive meal. The wine list is reasonably priced and extensive, with over 200 labels. All leading credit cards accepted.

HIGH STREET, CLAYGATE

RESERVATIONS:
TEL: ESHER (0372) 64882

THE ROSEBERY ROOM AT THE SOUTH HATCH RACING CLUB

Burgh Heath Road, Epsom. Tel: (037 27) 23204

Hours: *Open for lunch and dinner (last orders 9.45pm). Closed Sun evening/Mon.*

Average Prices: *A la Carte £16; Table d'Hôte lunch £11.75; Sun lunch £10.50. House wine £6.50 per bottle.*

Epsom, situated on the edge of the Epsom Downs, will always be synonymous with horse racing and its premier event, the Derby. Lord Rosebery, Liberal Prime Minister 1894–6 and the owner of a string of Derby winners, is recalled in the name of this restaurant which also houses a museum of racing memorabilia. Its elegant dining room is the setting for a traditional Anglo-French menu which begins with crevette chaud et salade d'ail (hot king prawns on a Continental salad with garlic) and feuilleté foie des volailles Madeira (sautéd chicken livers served on a puff pastry case with a Madeira sauce). Main course dishes include délice de sole cubat (sole poached in white wine, served on a mushroom duxelle and coated with a mild cheese sauce), rack of lamb with rosemary and medallions of venison with port. All dishes are home-made from local ingredients, including the desserts. There is also a varied cellar of carefully chosen wines. Private parties are catered for, with small wedding receptions a speciality.

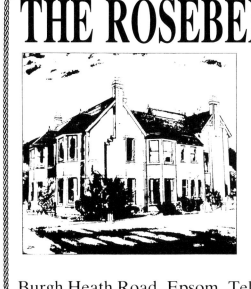

WOODLANDS PARK HOTEL

Woodlands Lane, Stoke D'Abernon, Cobham.
Tel: (037 284) 3933

Hours:	*Open for lunch and dinner. Closed Sat lunch.*
Average Prices:	*A la Carte £25; Table d'Hôte lunch £15, dinner £17.50.*
Wines:	*House wine £7.25 per bottle.*

Select Country Hotels have recently spent £6 million redeveloping and refurbishing this Victorian mansion into one of the most prestigious hotels in Surrey. With the highly successful Oak Room Restaurant, Woodlands Park has a new restaurant which has been carefully designed to recreate the splendour of the Victorian era. Trained at The Ritz, head chef Paul Jones has created exciting à la carte and table d'hôte selections. Try the fresh water crayfish tails and seasonal salad leaves with a warm truffle butter, followed by roast loin of English lamb in a mint crust on a rich ruby port sauce. Paula Banford, the pastry chef, learned her pâtissière's skills from the master himself, Michel Roux, and her selections of desserts are extremely appetising. There is also a wide selection of English cheeses and liqueurs to round off the meal. A resident pianist plays to diners from a minstrel's gallery, whilst accommodation is available in 59 en suite rooms and functions can be held in the oak-panelled Prince of Wales suite.

WOODLANDS PARK HOTEL   TEL: OXSHOTT (037 284) 3933

MOGUL DYNASTY

1 Craddocks Parade, Lower Ashtead.
Tel: (037 22) 74810/73627

Hours: *Open for lunch and dinner (last orders 11pm).*
Average Prices: A la Carte £12.50.
Wines: *House wine £6 per bottle.*

The Mogul Dynasty follows in the wake of its successful sister establishment, The Cannon Tandoori in Edgware, and has now been open for three years. Classical pillars, numerous pot plants and a refined cream décor create a sophisticated colonial atmosphere supportive of the quality of the cooking. Start with prawn with fresh pineapple (in season), or the chef's recommendation, tandoori lamb chops. The main course selection covers the full range, with tandooris — chicken saslick (marinated spring chicken barbecued on charcoal with green peppers, tomatoes and onions) — and curries — korma, Malaya, moglai, bhuna, dupiaza, to name but a few. There are also special curry dishes such as King Prawn Delight (king prawn cooked in mild cheese and fresh cream), jal frazi dishes (hot and spicy, cooked in wine vinegar with ginger, green chilli and green pepper) and other house specialities. The Mogul Special Moshala (on the bone chicken cooked with minced meat and oriental spices) is particularly popular.

MOGUL DYNASTY

A Restaurant that offers First Class Cuisine
in a warm, intimate, Eastern Atmosphere.
WEDDINGS AND PARTIES CATERED FOR. FULLY LICENSED.
Open seven days a week, including Bank Holidays
12 noon – 2.30pm   5.30pm – 11.00pm
For reservations tel: Ashtead (037 22) 74810 or 73627
1 CRADDOCKS PARADE · ASHTEAD · SURREY
Also: Cannon Tandoori, 7 Station Parade, Whitchurch Lane, Cannons Park,
Edgware, Middlesex. Tel: 01 952 2501 or 01 951 3965
Reservations advisable. All major credit cards accepted.

PIERROT RESTAURANT

20 Cheam Common Road, North Cheam.
Tel: (01) 337 5322/5611

Hours: *Open for lunch (last orders 2.30pm) and dinner (last orders 10.45pm). Closed Sun.*

Average Prices: *A la Carte £20.*

Wines: *House wine £6.95 per bottle.*

Pierrot dolls gaze down upon diners at this popular restaurant and add character to a building rich in beaming and copper artefacts. Its tables are neatly laid, with crisp linen and cut glass, and they seat 45 guests. Pre-dinner drinks are served from a cocktail bar, to be followed in the restaurant by an internationally-inspired menu, based on fresh market produce. Fish is a speciality and features prominently with shellfish, lobster and dishes such as salmon baked in the oven with filo pastry and a tomato and basil sauce. One popular stalwart of the menu is chicken Pierrot (chicken breast stuffed with monkfish, garlic and parsley in a light curry sauce). The accompanying wines number over 50 vintages and quality non-vintages. Prices are also sensible, appealing to a range of customers from businessmen to family diners. Although the restaurant is closed on Sunday for general trade, private parties are still catered for. All the major credit cards are accepted.

PIERROT
Restaurant

**Enjoy the Best
French & International
Cuisine in perfect surroundings**

20 Cheam Common Road
(by North Cheam traffic lights)
Worcester Park
Reservations: (01) 337 5322
(01) 337 5611

KELONG RESTAURANT

1 b–c Selsdon Road, South Croydon.
Tel: (01) 688 0726

Hours: *Open for lunch and dinner (last orders 10.45pm).*
Closed Sun.

Average Prices: *A la Carte £15.50; snacks £1.95.*

Wines: *House wine £6.50 per bottle.*

The tastes of Singapore, the food capital of Asia, are authentically recaptured in this lively restaurant which also offers Malaysian cuisine and has seafood as its speciality. The menu is vast but there are a number of varied price set menus to ease the problem of choice. Its highlight is the Steam Boat, for four people, which requires 24 hours' notice and is a kind of large fondue served with a selection of meat, seafood and vegetables. Begin with starters such as won-ton soup (pastry wrapped meat dumplings in soup) or seafood satay (skewers of marinated seafood with rice cakes, onion and a peanut-based sauce). The seafood selection for main course includes sections for squid, shellfish, prawns and fish. Here dishes such as drunken prawns (soaked in saké and fried with garlic, onions, and crushed peppercorns) and ikan assam pedas (fried mackerel, cooked in a spicy tamarind and pineapple sauce). Other options encompass noodle, rice, vegetarian and meat dishes. Singapore laska, for example, is a presentation of rice, vermicelli and yellow noodles in spicy coconut soup with shrimps, fishcake and beansprouts.

KELONG

MALAYSIAN SINGAPOREAN RESTAURANT

THE CEDAR HOUSE HOTEL AND DINING HALL

Mill Road, Cobham. Tel: (0932) 63424

Hours: *Open for dinner Tuesday–Saturday.*
Average Prices: *A la Carte £24; Table d'Hôte £16.95.*
Wines: *House wine £6.50 per bottle.*

Overlooking the River Mole and its surrounding watermeadows, The Cedar House Hotel dates back to the 15th century, although there have been many alterations since then. The house's Medieval origins are most strikingly displayed in the dining hall, which was first opened to non-residents in the autumn of 1988. Its high timbered ceiling, minstrel's gallery and leaded windows, which overlook the orchard garden, are softened by a peach colour scheme and candlelit tables. It is an atmospheric backdrop to the imaginative English-style menu of fresh seasonal produce. Typical starters include smoked salmon parcels filled with seafood, or wild mushrooms and fresh asparagus encased in puff pastry with a herb-scented hollandaise sauce. For a main course dish try the beef fillet with apple and Stilton, rolled in oats and cooked with a tomato and whisky sauce, or breast of duck with a honey and ginger sauce. Desserts are particularly tempting for the sweet-toothed, with walnut and treacle pudding, jam roly-poly or the more exotic white chocolate mousse topped with mango and pear. There is also a selection of British cheeses and a small but well-chosen wine list.

THE CEDAR HOUSE HOTEL AND DINING HALL

For fine seasonal food in an English style

Mill Road, Cobham   Telephone: Cobham (0932) 63424

VERMONT EXCHANGE

46 Portsmouth Road, Cobham.
Tel: (0932) 62015

Hours:	*Open for lunch and dinner.*
Average Prices:	*A la Carte £10.95; snacks from £2.50.*
Wines:	*House wine £6.25 per bottle.*

Vermont Exchange is a fun and lively restaurant which invites its customers to sizzle Mexican-style or 'boogie on down' to the deep South. The menu is large and begins with appetisers such as battered calamari (succulent slices of deep-fried squid) and breaded zucchini (deep-fried courgette wheels). Hot and spicy Cajun cooking features on the main course, where there is shark steak Cajun-style, in an avocado sauce, and Eastern chicken for a more oriental taste. In addition, there are many Tex-Mex favourites such as loaded skins, chicken wings, ribs and burgers. For the very hungry there is the 'Big Mouth' (14 ounces of pure beef). Desserts are rich and chocolatey with the popular Death by Chocolate, as well as Chocolate Monkey, a hybrid drink/dessert. There are cocktails a plenty, including the infamous Vermont cocktail, and an international selection of beers and wines. The Vermont Exchange is an ideal venue for families and parties, all professionally catered for.

COBHAM TANDOORI RESTAURANT

12c Anyards Road, Cobham.
Tel: (0932) 63842/66036

Hours: *Open for lunch and dinner (last orders 11.15pm).*
Average Prices: *A la Carte £10.*
Wines: *House wine £5.50 per bottle.*

The great attraction of The Cobham Tandoori Restaurant is that it presents truly authentic Indian dishes cooked as they would be at home. The emphasis is quality before quantity, but the menu is still ample in its coverage. To begin try shami kebab (specially fried lamb, finely trimmed and flavoured with herbs and spices), chicken chat (small juicy pieces of chicken, hot and sour) or perhaps chilled melon, for a more refreshing appetiser to the palate. The main course covers tandoori, chicken and lamb specialities, seafood, Persian and biriani dishes. Regular favourites here include chingri jhoi (prawns Bengali-style), chicken or lamb korai (medium hot, cooked with herbs, spices and tomatoes and served in an iron korai), or lamb rogon josh (medium hot lamb cooked with tomatoes and green peppers in a spicy sauce). For dessert, try gulab jamon (curd cheese with a little flour, fried in ghee and served in syrup). All dishes are served by waiters in traditional kurta shirts, with the atmospheric surroundings of the restaurant adding to the well-rounded enjoyment of the meal. Booking is recommended at the weekend.

THE CRICKETERS

Downside, Cobham. Tel: (0932) 62105

Hours:	*Open for coffee, lunch and dinner (last orders 10pm). Restaurant closed Sun evening/Mon.*
Average Prices:	*A la Carte £18; Sun lunch £8.50; snacks from £1.95.*
Wines:	*House wine £6.45 per carafe; £3.35 per half-carafe.*

Run by Brian and Wendy Luxford, The Cricketers is a highly traditional pub with very low beaming and a number of horse brasses. In the elegant restaurant exposed brickwork ensures character and quality napery and cut glass add refinement. The menu mixes English and French styles, with starters such as French onion soup, escargots, stuffed smoked fillet of trout and melon with sorbet. The main course covers a range of steak, poultry, fish and vegetarian dishes and there are several chef's specials of the day. Typical of the choice is carpetbagger steak, chicken cacciatora, loin of pork with a prune sauce, and salmon with a cream of tarragon sauce. For afters the trolley is laden with sweets and, to accompany, a thoughtfully-compiled wine list, covering 50 labels, is offered. As an alternative, try the cold buffet with its inexpensive, but enticing dishes. Much thought has been put into this inn to maintain a careful balance between old and new. The attractive garden is full of flowers and the inn itself faces open commonland. Children are made very welcome and an area is set aside for their use.

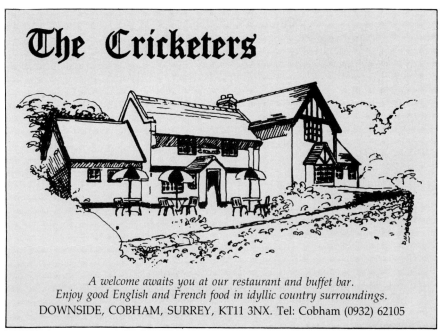

The Cricketers

A welcome awaits you at our restaurant and buffet bar.
Enjoy good English and French food in idyllic country surroundings.
DOWNSIDE, COBHAM, SURREY, KT11 3NX. Tel: Cobham (0932) 62105

IL GIARDINO

221 Portsmouth Road, Cobham. Tel: (0932) 63973

Hours: *Open for lunch and dinner. Closed Sat lunch/Mon.*

Average Prices: *A la Carte £20.50; Table d'Hôte £9.50.*

Gabriele Di Michele, the proprietor of Il Giardino, has created a restaurant highly reminiscent of an Italian terrace garden. Wrought iron, terracotta and ceramics create a pleasant backdrop to specialities such as scaloppine di vitello al granchio e avocado (veal escalope with crab meat and avocado in a cream and tomato sauce) and agnello scottaditta (lamb cutlet cooked with garlic, chilli and rosemary).

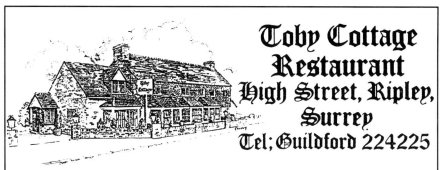

Toby Cottage Restaurant
High Street, Ripley, Surrey
Tel; Guildford 224225

Hours: *Open for lunch and dinner.*
                 Closed Sun evening/Mon.

Average Prices: A la Carte £12–£16; Table d'Hôte £9; wine £7.

For the best in English and French cuisine dine in this charming old 16th century restaurant. A delightful spot for that special occasion, relax with a drink in the spacious cocktail bar and dine in style from the extensive à la carte menu, or choose one of the speciality dishes of the day. Sunday lunch is also available and private parties and weddings catered for. For further information telephone Guildford (0483) 224225

THE NORTHFLEET HOTEL

Claremont Avenue, Woking. Tel: (048 62) 22971

Hours:	*Open for coffee, lunch, tea and dinner (last orders 9.15pm, 9.30pm Fri/Sat). Closed Sun evening.*
Average Prices:	*A la Carte £13; Sun lunch £7.95; snacks from £1.25.*
Wines:	*House wine £5.75 per bottle.*

Ten minutes from the centre of Woking is a hotel which reflects the peacefulness of the suburbs in which it is set. The hotel has 25 airy and light bedrooms and The Avenue Restaurant, which has a relaxed and unhurried atmosphere. Hot or cold hors d'oeuvre to begin include ravioli alla casalinga (home-made ravioli served with a mushroom and tomato sauce) and prawn caprice (half ogen melon filled with prawns and topped with mayonnaise). For the main course there are fish, grills, meats and poultry dishes. Choose between suprême de sole Phillipe (fillets of sole with a white wine and prawn sauce), blancs de volaille au sabayon de poireau (chicken breasts stuffed and perfumed with leeks), celestine de boeuf au poivre vert (strips of beef in a cream sauce with green peppercorns) or entrecôte grillée (grilled sirloin steak garnished with game chips). Desserts from the trolley and a selection of cheeses conclude. For lighter meals or snacks, or a pint of real ale, try the friendly bar. All the major credit cards are accepted.

SOONS

1 St John's Road, Woking.
Tel: (048 62) 26290

Hours: *Open for lunch and dinner (last orders 10.30pm).*
Average Prices: *A la Carte £15; chef's special Table d'Hôte £13.75.*
Wines: *House wine £5.95 per bottle.*

A smart contemporary décor characterizes Soons Restaurant. A high spotlit ceiling looks down upon tables which are decorated in soft pink with a flurry of fresh and dry flowers and surrounded by elegant ladderback chairs. The air-conditioned restaurant is always busy and specialises in Pekinese and Szechuan cooking, detailed on a comprehensive four page menu. Curried wan tun (a crispy ravioli), Manchurian lamb or sesame prawns could begin, followed, perhaps, by aromatic duck as an intermediate course. For a main course dish try Szechuan specialities like crispy beef with carrot and chilli, sea spice chicken or squid with a black bean sauce. Glazed toffee apple then makes an appetising and traditional end to the meal. As well as the oriental selections, there are also some 30 Continental wines. All the major credit cards are accepted and private parties are catered for. Open seven days a week.

Soons

信仕京菜

FINE PEKING AND SZECHUAN CUISINE

AIR CONDITIONED WATERSIDE DINING

OPEN 7 DAYS A WEEK FOR LUNCH AND DINNER

1 ST JOHN'S ROAD, WOKING. TEL: WOKING (04862) 26290

FOXHILLS

Stonehill Road, Ottershaw. Tel: (093 287) 2050

Hours: *Open for coffee, lunch, tea and dinner (last orders 10pm). Closed Sun evening/Mon lunch.*

Average Prices: *A la Carte £20; executive lunch £12.50.*

Wines: *House wine £7.95 per bottle.*

Foxhills combines the traditional splendour and comforts of a country mansion with a range of sporting facilities to test the most ardent of enthusiasts. It is, in essence, a country club conceived on a grand scale and with ready accessibility, being close to the M25. Its Manor Restaurant overlooks 400 acres of parkland and has a high vaulted ceiling, the dark oak of which provides a striking contrast to the apricot furnishings. The menu is international and seasonal, offering starters such as mousse of avocado (surrounded with smoked salmon and sliced avocado, floated on a yoghurt and poppyseed dressing). Main course dishes are equally inventive with, for example, slices of grilled calves' liver and smoked bacon, garnished with a saffron flavoured apple and shallot compote, and, for vegetarians, a savoury choux pastry ring filled with broccoli and mushrooms, served with a grain mustard sauce and finished with flaked almonds. For dessert try the sharp raspberry and cognac cream served on a biscuit tulip, covered with a sugar cage on a raspberry coulis. Buffet-style Sunday lunch with over 40 dishes.

ASKEW'S RESTAURANT

15 Bishopsmead Parade, East Horsley.
Tel: (048 65) 4484/2024

Hours: *Open for lunch and dinner (last orders 10pm).*
             Closed Sunday evening/Mon.
Average Prices: *A la Carte £16; Table d'Hôte £8.50; Sun lunch £9.50.*
Wines: *House wine £5.95 per bottle.*

Askew's is decorated in peaches and cream with an abundance of plants and a small bar area for pre-dinner drinks. Since taking over her own restaurant three years ago, Hazel Askew, the chef-proprietor, has been steadily building up an ever-widening reputation for simply cooked and appetising cuisine. There is no pretension but plenty of quality on the international menu, which offers dishes where the natural flavours of food are allowed to speak for themselves. Starters include king prawns grilled in garlic butter and rolled in bacon, and Stilton soup. The main course features game in season, a range of steaks, an extremely popular steak and kidney pie and dishes such as Dover sole, crab au gratin and duckling off the bone with a green pepper sauce. For dessert try some lemon Cotswold, peaches in brandy, or crêpes Suzette. The wine list is extensive, with prominent Burgundies. The table d'hôte menu is reckoned excellent value and has proved popular with the business community. Once a month there is also a special vegetarian night.

15 Bishopsmead Parade, East Horsley, Surrey KT24 6RT

★ English and Continental Cuisine

★ Fully Licensed   ★ Convenient Parking

★ Extensive Wine List

★ Business Lunches *catering to your company requirements*

TELEPHONE (04865) 4484 & 2024

THATCHERS RESORT HOTEL

Epsom Road, East Horsley.
Tel: (048 65) 4291

Hours: *Open for coffee, lunch, tea and dinner (last orders 10pm, 9.30pm Sun). Bar meals lunchtime.*

Average Prices: *A la Carte £25; Table d'Hôte £15; Sun lunch £13.50.*

Wines: *House wine £6.95 per bottle.*

Set back off the A246, which runs along the northern edge of the downs, is a hotel with an appealing half-timbered Tudor-style façade, surrounded by inviting flower-filled gardens. It was fashionable during the 1920's as an upmarket tearoom and has since developed into a comfortably English hotel. The cooking, however, under head chef Mark Mench, is decidedly French with, for example, mousse de foie de volaille en brioche (smooth chicken liver mousse, studded with pistachio nuts and truffles, encased in brioche pastry), or hot goat's cheese salad, for a starter. Main courses include suprême de saumon farci, sauce au Madère (fillet of salmon stuffed with a fish mousse and served in a Madeira butter and chive sauce). The highlight of the dessert menu is the tulipe Escoffier (brandy snap basket dipped in chocolate and filled with whipped cream and fresh fruits). Bar meals do not stint on flair either, with savoury pancakes stuffed with vegetable ratatouille, for vegetarians, and breast of chicken stuffed with avocado and baked in cream.

MORPHOU RESTAURANT

Guildford Road, Bookham. Tel: (0372) 59256/842895

Hours: *Open for lunch and dinner (last orders 10.30pm). Closed Sat lunch/Sun.*

Average Prices: *A la Carte £18; Table d'Hôte lunch £10.50, dinner £16.50. House wine £6.75 per bottle.*

Morphou Restaurant is situated on the main A246 Bookham–Guildford road. It is a family-run restaurant, decorated in pastel pinks and creams, with exposed beaming, crisp white table linen and finely cut glassware. The cooking is French-Greek and the menu interesting. Starters include Stilton and Brie Morphou (fried in filo pastry, served with sherried grapes and a cranberry sauce) and avocado pear Flasher (avocado pear filled with fresh crabmeat, avalanched with lobster and a brandy sauce and baked). The main course divides itself into poissons, entrées and grillades. Typical of the selection here is scampi biarotte (pan-fried with shallots, tarragon and mushrooms, and glazed with a lobster and brandy sauce and timbale of rice), confit of duckling filfar (half duckling boned and finished in an orange liqueur sauce with fresh fruit basket) and tournedos forestière (middle cut fillet, pan-fried with wild mushrooms and baby vegetables in a Madeira meat glaze). For an alternative to the usual crêpes Suzette, try crêpes Andres (filled with vanilla ice cream and garnished with roasted almonds).

BOOKHAM GRANGE HOTEL'S POLESDEN ROOM RESTAURANT

Little Bookham Common, Bookham.
Tel: (0372) 52742/52743

Hours:	*Open for coffee, lunch, tea and dinner.*
Average Prices:	*A la Carte £13.50; Table d'Hôte £9.90; snacks from 95p.*
Wines:	*House wine £5.75 per bottle.*

Bookham Grange is a hotel which retains all the charm of an old English house. Fresh flowers, low beaming and autumnal colours conjure a particularly countrified atmosphere in The Polesden Room Restaurant which serves a varied Continental menu. Start with spicy stuffed mushrooms (mushrooms stuffed with pâté, golden fried with a spicy mayonnaise), or scallops Mornay (lightly poached with a cheese sauce). There is a choice of about 13 dishes for the main course and these cover steak Madagascar (prime fillet steak sautéed with peppercorns, flamed in brandy and finished with cream), rack of lamb Gainsborough (best end of lamb with a light redcurrant and rosemary gravy) and scampi Newburg (scampi simmered in a lobster sauce with mushrooms and brandy). For dessert try some baked Alaska or pineapple surprise (quarter of pineapple with dairy ice cream and crushed pineapple) and, to conclude, a liqueur coffee. Bar meals are also available, whilst receptions and other functions can be held in the Eastwick or Wedgwood Rooms.

Bookham Grange Hotel

LITTLE BOOKHAM COMMON, BOOKHAM, LEATHERHEAD
Telephone: Bookham 52742/3

45

CARLETON'S RESTAURANT

Highland Cottage, Junction Road, Dorking.
Tel: (0306) 888608

Hours: *Open for lunch and dinner (last orders 10pm,*
10.30pm Fri/Sat). Closed Sun/Mon.

Average Prices: *Lunch from £10.25; dinner £17.*

Wines: *House wine £5.50 per bottle.*

Carleton Smith's recently-opened restaurant has already established a clear identity, as a place where choice, but simply presented dishes are offered against an informal but elegant background. The latter is characterized by exposed brickwork, crisp pink table linen and sprigs of fresh flowers, whilst the style of cooking is English with French leanings. Quality is put before quantity and the menu choice, therefore, is not extensive. Starters begin with roulade of chicken filled with garlic, leek and pistachio, served on a brioche, or spiced rare beef with a coconut salad. Local seasonal ingredients compose the main course, which offers roast loin of English lamb marinated in mint, coriander and lemon juice, served with a tamarind sauce, and a pair of roast boneless quails with a chestnut and duck sausage and a sultana and port gravy. There is a separate dessert menu which changes regularly and features some appetising pastries. The setting is an ideal one for business lunches when the menu may include salmon escalope baked en papillote with a dill hollandaise sauce.

carleton's restaurant

Highland Cottage, Junction Road, Dorking
Tel: Dorking (0306) 888608

THE BURFORD BRIDGE HOTEL

Box Hill, Dorking. Tel: (0306) 884561

Hours:	*Open for coffee, lunch, afternoon tea and dinner (last orders 9.30pm).*
Average Prices:	*A la Carte £25; Table d'Hôte lunch £16.50, dinner £17.50.*
Wines:	*House wine £10.75 per bottle.*

The expanse of the Box Hill downlands surrounds this white-fronted hotel which dates in the main part back to the 18th century. Many famous guests have stayed here, including Keats, who was inspired to write *Endymion* in one of its rooms overlooking the gardens. Today, period antiques, fresh flowers and a tranquil setting combine to give it a very English atmosphere that is reflected in its seasonally changing menu. Appetisers begin with salmon tartare (tartare of fresh and smoked salmon with caviar), terrine of foie gras (home-made goose liver terrine with baby leeks, accompanied with brioche) and shellfish consommé (flavoured with lemon grass and garnished with fresh shellfish). Main course dishes include sea bass oriental (with spring onions, ginger and soy sauce), breast of duck (pan-fried with an onion confit and grenadine) and rack of lamb persillade for two people (boned and rolled lamb filled with garlic herbs, breadcrumbs and pot-roasted). Desserts are from the trolley and there is a selection of English and French cheeses. Coffee and tea with petits fours add the finishing touches.

The Burford Bridge

at the foot of Box Hill, Dorking, Surrey RH5 6BX.
Tel: Dorking (0306) 884561. Telex: 859507. Fax: (0306) 880386.

SEVEN STARS LEIGH

Leigh, near Reigate. Tel: (030 678) 254

Hours: *Open for coffee, lunch and dinner.*

Average Prices: *A la Carte £5 (2 courses); bar snacks 75p–£6.50.*

Wines: *House wine £5.50 per bottle; £1 per glass.*

The village of Leigh, straddling the River Mole, can be found three miles off the A25 Dorking-Reigate road in a notably attractive stretch of countryside. The Seven Stars has an ancient lineage which extends back to the 14th century. Beside its old inglenook fireplace, for example, there is placard displaying a welcome for drinkers from the landlord — dated 1637. An extensive lunchtime and evening menu is available seven days a week and personally supervised by today's landlord. Dishes such as moussaka, chicken tikka, lasagne verdi and chilli con carne are all home-cooked, with other specialities including steak and kidney pie, vegetarian dishes such as vegetable casserole and spinach and cheese lasagne, and fish, steaks, gammon and mixed grills. Desserts are also home-made and include blackcurrant and apple pie and lemon meringue pie. Outside is a lovely garden, with tables shaded by umbrellas, which offers steaks and chicken from a barbecue every summer weekend (weather permitting), together with a help-yourself salad bar. This is a Friary Meux pub and has Best Bitter, Burton and John Bull Cask Bitter all on tap.

Pleasant food in pleasant surroundings.
LEIGH, NR. REIGATE
Telephone: Dawes Green (030 678) 254

NUTFIELD PRIORY

Nutfield Priory, Nutfield, Redhill.
Tel: (0737) 822066

Hours: *Open for lunch, 12.30–2pm, and dinner, 7–10pm.*
Average Prices: *A la Carte £23.*
Wines: *House wine £8.*

Nutfield Priory is a charming country house hotel which sits high on a ridge and commands superb views across the Surrey weald. It was built between 1872 and 1874 for Joshua Fielden MP in a Tudor style and today the elegance and grandeur of a bygone age can still be enjoyed within its walls. In particular, the unique cloistered restaurant, with its vaulted ceiling arching gently upwards, and the lead-light windows, makes an impressive setting for any occasion. Described as 'the best of modern English', the cuisine is imaginatively prepared by Head Chef Martin Bradley. The beauty of nouvelle cuisine is offered, but with portions ample enough to satisfy the most demanding of appetites. To complement the food, there is a large cellar which holds both vintage wines and finer examples from other years. The staff are professional and friendly, offering advice and guidance where necessary. Functions ranging from wedding receptions to conferences and private dinner parties are all catered for.

NUTFIELD PRIORY

Superb Cuisine : Fine Wines : Elegant Surroundings

For your reservation please call
(0737) 822066
Nutfield Priory, Nutfield, Redhill, Surrey RH1 4EN

THE OLD LODGE AT LIMPSFIELD

	High Street, Limpsfield. Tel: (0883) 714365
Hours:	*Open for coffee, lunch, tea and dinner (last orders 10.30pm). Closed Sun evening/Mon.*
Average Prices:	*A la Carte £20; Table d'Hôte lunch £13.50; Sun lunch £14.50.*
Wines:	*House wine £6.50 per bottle.*

Limpsfield is one of a string of attractive villages which lie along the A25 at the foot of the North Downs. The Old Lodge has been converted from its original 19th century building and still retains many of its original features. A high vaulted ceiling, oak panelling, an impressive old fireplace and lattice windows create a traditional and relaxing setting in which to enjoy the French cooking of the chef. Brie with a gooseberry sauce, and oyster mushrooms stuffed with crab are both available for starters. Fish is a speciality of the menu with such dishes as scampi rolled in smoked salmon and sole fillet poached in champagne with a lobster sauce. There is also a range of steaks, game in season and English dishes like rack of lamb with mustard. Desserts are all home-made — profiteroles, cheesecake, pies, gâteaux and more. The accompanying wines are from Europe and cover 50 labels. The comfortable lounge offers relaxation before or after meals and private parties for up to 100 can be catered for. Major credit cards accepted.

Gatwick Penta Hotel

Povey Cross Road,
Horley, Surrey RH6 0BE
Tel: (0293) 820169

Hours:	*Open for lunch and dinner (last orders 10.45pm).*
Average Prices:	*A la Carte £17; Table d'Hôte £14.50; Sun lunch £10.50.*
Wines:	*House wine £7.75 per bottle.*

Situated deliberately close to Gatwick airport, The Gatwick Penta is geared to providing a 24 hour service and a range of amenities to divert and refresh jaded air travellers. A leisure centre (with gym, saunas and jacuzzi) and a round the clock coffee shop are just two of the facilities on offer. The Pavilion Restaurant, in keeping with the rest of the hotel, is spacious, modern and relaxing. The menu is traditional and nouvelle, changing with the four seasons. Starters include exotic melon accompanied by a light sweet redcurrant purée, and jumbo scallops wrapped in pastry, oven-baked and served on a delicate spinach sauce. The main course covers a number of grill dishes, chef's specialities and stir-fried specialities. Try dishes such as strips of beef fillet (stir-fried with bamboo shoots, beansprouts, peppers and onion with rice), breast of pheasant (coated in nut crumble, pan-fried and dressed on a dark wine sauce), or pork medallions (pan-fried with garlic, presented with soy sauce and a Chinese leaf salad). Cocktails are served in the Brighton Belle bar.

effingham park

The Wellingtonia offers an extensive selection from the Carte du Jour, and is ideal for the Business Executive if time is of the essence.

The Wellingtonia à la carte restaurant

The Wellingtonia is not the only facility available at Effingham Park; after your meal it is possible to enjoy a relaxing walk through the gardens, or for the more energetic we have our own 9 hole Golf Course (nominal green fees apply), Putting Green, Croquet Lawn and extensive Leisure Club with swimming pool, saunas, jacuzzi and Turkish Baths — day membership is available to visitors.

EFFINGHAM PARK, WEST PARK ROAD, COPTHORNE, WEST SUSSEX.
Restaurant: (0342) 717559   Hotel: (0342) 714994

EFFINGHAM PARK

West Park Road, Copthorne.
Tel: (0342) 717559/714994

Hours:	*Open for lunch and dinner. Restaurant closed Sat lunch/all day Sun.*
Average Prices:	*A la Carte £20; Carte du Jour £13.50.*
Wines:	*House wine £9.25 per bottle.*

Effingham Park, which opened in September 1988, is a hotel which aims to make business and leisure a pleasure, and preferably the two in tandem. 40 acres of parkland, a wealth of amenities (including a leisure club, a croquet lawn and a nine hole golf course) and a design on a grand scale contribute to a striking first impression. The Wellingtonia has its own separate entrance and is named after the Wellingtonia trees which line its driveway. The décor is relaxing and modern; elegance is the keynote. Large, delicately arched windows, which overlook the gardens, and pale pink napery create a relaxing backdrop to the culinary skills of the team of chefs who present a selection of dishes à la carte, as well as a carte du jour. The hotel is located on B2028, half a mile off the main A264 and close to junction 10 of the M23.

THE SUN INN

The Common, Dunsfold.
Tel: (048 649) 242

Hours: *Open for coffee, lunch and dinner (last orders 10pm).*

Average Prices: *A la Carte £11.75; Sun lunch £8.75; snacks £1.25.*

Wines: *House wine £5.25 per bottle.*

Dunsfold, one of the attractive fold villages, provides a peaceful setting for the 17th century Sun Inn, which overlooks the village cricket green. It has inspired tenant Judith Dunne, with the help of her chef, Robert Cooke, to create an interesting menu, utilising fresh meat, fish and vegetables. Cooking is both English and French in style, with an extensive blackboard menu which changes daily. Some of the popular and regularly featuring snacks and dishes are steak and kidney pie, delicious fish cakes, local seasonal game such as venison, pigeon and rabbit and summer fresh seafood specials with Dover sole, lobster and Mediterranean prawns. The restaurant serves a weekly-changing à la carte selection. Typical dishes here include chicken breast stuffed with Brie and served with an apricot sauce, and sautéed monkfish with white wine, tomato and basil. The garden holds summer barbecues and there is an old hop bar available for private hire. Major credit cards accepted.

T
H
E

S
U
N

I
N
N

THE COMMON, DUNSFOLD. TELEPHONE: DUNSFOLD 048649-242

THE CROWN INN

The Green, Chiddingfold.
Tel: (042 879) 2255

Hours: *Open for coffee, lunch, tea and dinner (last orders 9.30pm).*

Average Prices: *A la Carte £20; Table d'Hôte £12; snacks from £2.*

Wines: *House wine £7 per bottle.*

A licence extending back to 1383, an equally historic interior and a setting on the village green make The Crown all that one could hope for in a village inn. The past is overwhelming, with massive beaming, dark panelling, an ornately carved fireplace and a coin collection dating back four centuries. Both Edward VI and Elizabeth I are believed to have stayed at the inn, whilst today's customers are attracted by quality English cuisine, as well as the atmosphere. Typical of the seasonal dishes on offer are fillet of beef, pan-fried and served with a noodle basket of wild mushrooms and light Madeira jus, and safari of fish and shellfish steamed in their own juices with an oyster-flavoured sauce. Desserts are equally as tempting, with, for example, a dark chocolate, rum and raisin mousse, and a crisp biscuit tulip. Real ales are on tap in The Huntsman's Bar where there is also a choice between snacks, full meals and afternoon tea. In summer sitting outside on the green is a real pleasure; the enjoyment of a drink whilst surveying the movement of village life.

THE CROWN INN

THE GREEN
CHIDDINGFOLD

HARMONY INNS
THE INDIVIDUAL INNS

TEL: WORMLEY (042879) 2255/6

LYTHE HILL HOTEL AND RESTAURANTS

Petworth Road, Haslemere.
Tel: (0428) 51251

Hours: *Auberge de France open for dinner, Tues–Sun, and Sun lunch. Closed Mon. Lythe Hill Restaurant open for lunch and dinner. Closed Sat evening/Sun lunch.*

Average Prices: *A la Carte from £20, Table d'Hôte £17.50 (Auberge de France); A la Carte/Table d'Hôte £14.50 (Lythe Hill Restaurant). Sun lunch £16.*

Wines: *House wine £8.50 per bottle.*

Lythe Hill has a romantic and immediately appealing situation, standing on the slope of a hill and surrounded by 14 acres of sculptured gardens with an ornamental lake. The two main buildings face one another across the car park; one a black and white half timbered farmhouse, the setting for the Auberge de France; the other the main hotel with its own restaurant.

The Auberge de France has both elegance and charm. The oak beamed dining room, with its inglenook fireplace and polished oak tables, adjoins a cocktail bar and terrace which overlook the attractive gardens. The restaurant has long been renowned for its classical cuisine and has recently introduced an exciting new menu, offering specialities such as Dover sole with a lemon and chervil mousse in a wine and cream sauce, and venison served with juniper berries on a Burgundy sauce. The chef also produces some unusual combinations such as river trout and monkfish in a champagne sauce, and trio of lamb, beef and veal in a wine sauce. On the menu for dessert are crêpes Suzette and hot soufflés.

The accompanying wine list is extensive, with over 200 wines from more than a dozen countries and many quality vintages from famous châteaux and wine growing areas of France.

Across the courtyard and under the pigeon loft is the main hotel restaurant, decorated in soft tones of pink and blue with a refreshingly countrified atmosphere that makes an ideal partner for the imaginative English cooking of chef Roger Clark. Both à la carte and table d'hôte selections are wide-ranging and use the finest local ingredients brought daily from the markets.

The whole hotel complex has been recently refurbished and now caters for all manner of functions from wedding receptions to private dinner parties and banquets. There are also two purpose-built conference suites and a variety of smaller meeting rooms.

SHRIMPTON'S LICENSED RESTAURANT

Kingsley Green, Haslemere. Tel: (0428) 3539

Hours:	*Open for lunch and dinner (last orders 9.45pm).*
	Closed Sat lunch/Sun.
Average Prices:	*A la Carte £19.50; set lunch £11.50.*
Wines:	*House wine £7.50 per bottle.*

Situated on the A286 Haslemere–Midhurst road is a restaurant recommended by many food experts for its imaginative cuisine and engaging 16th century setting. A new chef has also brought a fresh approach to the restaurant's Anglo-French cuisine, resulting in a menu of inventive dishes with light, subtle sauces and attractive presentation. For starter there is coffre de champignons sauvages (wild mushrooms cooked in a white wine and garlic sauce and served in a pastry case), or flétan fumé au sauce crème coriandre (smoked Greenland halibut with a sour cream, dill and coriander sauce). As usual, generous portions are the rule for main course dishes such as saumon en habit vert à la nage de coquillages (steamed salmon wrapped in spinach and served with a mussel and cream sauce), or filet aux deux sauces (pan-fried fillet steak covered with a rich red wine sauce and a Stilton and spring onion sauce). Tempting desserts include strawberry and pineapple Romanoff and torta de bosque (cream pâtisserie piled high with different berries). Separate cocktail lounge upstairs.

MORELS

25–27 Lower Street, Haslemere. Tel: (0428) 51462

Hours: *Open for lunch and dinner (last orders 10pm).*
Closed Sun/Mon.

Average Prices: *A la Carte £25; Table d'Hôte lunch £14, dinner £17.*

Wines: *House wine £9 per bottle.*

Since 1980, when Jean-Yves Morel and his wife, Mary-Anne, opened up a listed 300-year-old building as a restaurant, they have been continually refining its service and style, a process which has culminated in a string of culinary awards. Morels has the atmosphere of a family dining room: elegant, but not imposing. A lounge has recently been added, giving diners the chance to peruse the menu before being seated. The selection of dishes changes monthly and is seasonally based. The starter list, however, usually includes blini (Russian pancake with smoked salmon, caviar and sour cream) which has been a favourite since the restaurant's early days. The main course in spring might offer filet d'agneau et sa panouffle au basilic, son jus (best English spring lamb topped with a basil mousseline and served with the pan juice). Dessert sees an interesting variation on crème brûlée — crème Grandmère, served with fresh fruit and home-made sorbet. The wine list covers 120 labels and is mainly French. Jean-Yves himself is well-known for his approachability and often intermingles with guests at the end of the evening.

CROWN'S

Weyhill, Haslemere. Tel: (0428) 3112
Hours: *Open for coffee, lunch and dinner.*
Average Prices: A la Carte £12; Sun lunch £5.95; snacks from £1.50.
Under the personal care of Brenda Heath for the past 13 years, Crown's has achieved an enviable reputation for its home-cooked food. A daily blackboard shows pasta dishes, imaginative vegetarian recipes and plenty of meat and seafood, for example poached baby salmon with a mild lemon sauce. Tasty and rich puddings include a special and popular treacle tart. Good varied wine list. Real ales. Pretty garden. Parking.

One of the best eating
places in Surrey

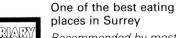

*Recommended by most
major food guides*

WEYHILL, HASLEMERE
TEL: (0428) 3112

SAN JOSE RESTAURANT

Chelmsford House Hotel, Haslemere Road, Fernhurst.
Tel: (0428) 53497
Hours: *Open for lunch and dinner (last orders 10pm).*
Average Prices: A la Carte £13.50; Table d'Hôte £8.75; Sun lunch £9.25.
Wines: *House wine £5.50 per bottle.*
Proprietor Jose Mora Afonso has recreated the tastes and atmosphere of Spain in the dining room of Chelmsford House Hotel. The room is light and airy, with arched windows overlooking the gardens and tables decorated in pink with sprigs of fresh flowers. There are regular speciality evenings when a completely Spanish, Italian or French menu is served, but the general menu itself is Continentally-varied. Gravad lax with a mild mustard sauce and paupiette de saumon fumé aux crevettes (smoked salmon rolled with prawns in a cocktail sauce) are both available for a starter, followed by main course dishes such as zarzuela de pescado (selection of fish and shellfish in a white wine provençale sauce) and tournado al estilo de Dijon (fillet steak served with a mild Dijon mustard, white wine and chive sauce). The specialities of the house are the flambé dishes, prepared at the table, and these range from exotic scampi to medallions of beef. Desserts feature crème caramel, pineapple gondolas and oranges in Grand Marnier. Private parties of up to 70 catered for. The hotel itself is small and friendly.

THE BISHOP'S TABLE RESTAURANT

West Street, Farnham.
Tel: (0252) 710222

Hours: *Open for lunch and dinner. Closed Sat lunch.*

Average Prices: *A la Carte £20; Table d'Hôte £12.50; vegetarian £13.50.*

Wines: *House wine £6.25 per bottle.*

The elegant Bishop's Table Restaurant dates back to the early 1700's, presenting a pleasant Georgian facade and with a beautifully landscaped, secluded walled garden, dominated by its massive cedar tree to the rear. It was originally owned by the Marquis of Lothian and now, as a restaurant, it enjoys a splendid reputation locally and places great emphasis on providing a personal but unobtrusive service. It is ideally located for a meal before or after the theatre and offers an imaginative à la carte selection and a tempting table d'hôte menu. There is also a separate vegetarian menu with a wide choice of hors d'oeuvre and entrées. Diners have the chance to peruse the menu whilst relaxing in the comfortable bar lounge where pre-dinner drinks whet the appetite. The Bishop's Table is also available for wedding receptions, dinner parties, business functions and other celebrations.

THE
BISHOP'S TABLE
RESTAURANT
27 West Street   Farnham   Surrey   GU9 7DR
Telephone: (0252) 710222

KAR LING KWONG RESTAURANT

48–50 East Street, Farnham.
Tel: (0252) 714854

Hours: *Open for lunch (last orders 2pm, 3pm Sun) and dinner (last orders 11.30pm).*

Average Prices: *A la Carte £9–£15.*

Wines: *House wine £8 per bottle.*

Henry Liu, the proprietor of Kar Ling Kwong, first entered the restaurant trade in 1964, in response to the lack of authentic Chinese restaurants of a high quality outside the centre of London. He saw no reason why this was the case, as both high quality ingredients and Chinese flavourings were readily available, and so decided to set up his own business in Farnham. Since that time his restaurant has remained an education in oriental tastes, with his skilled chef providing dishes attractive in colour, fragrant in aroma and contrasting in flavours. Service is still friendly and efficient, even extending to lessons in the art of using chopsticks. The menu itself covers many familiar dishes, as well as a select speciality list. The set meals are value for money and handy for those who do not wish to unravel the main menu. There is also a vegetarian menu, offering half a dozen dishes at a fixed price. The restaurant has recently been extended and refurbished, and now caters for private parties and conferences.

THE DARJEELING

25 South Street, Farnham.
Tel: (0252) 714322

Hours: *Open for lunch and dinner (last orders 11.30pm).*
Average Prices: *A la Carte £14.*
Wines: *House wine £5.95 per bottle.*

Elegantly lit archways, chandeliered lighting and decorative Indian brasses and prints all contribute to the atmosphere of The Darjeeling which has been steadily extending its reputation since its opening two years ago. There is a small cocktail bar in which to peruse the menu on which traditional coverage of Indian cuisine is enlivened by a number of chef's specialities. Begin, perhaps, with shashlick chicken (diced chicken specially marinated with tomatoes, onion and green pepper, barbecued and served on skewers), or the unusual Trout Delight (trout marinated in a subtle sauce and barbecued). For a main course dish there is a karahi chicken tikka (chicken tikka marinated in a specially prepared thick sauce, cooked and served on a cast iron dish and garnished with onions and tomatoes), and Darjeeling Special (diced spring chicken marinated with yoghurt in subtle spices and served on sizzling skewers with tomatoes, onions and green peppers). The range of side dishes and sundries includes peshwari nan (nan stuffed with dry fruits) and tarka dal (spiced lentils with fried garlic).

The Darjeeling

for the finest Indian Cuisine

Lunch 12–2pm
Evening 6–11.30pm
7 days a week

25 South Street
Farnham
Reservations
Tel: Farnham
(0252)
714322

SEVENS WINE BAR AND BISTRO

7 The Borough, Farnham. Tel: (0252) 715345

Hours: *Open for coffee, lunch, tea and dinner (last orders 11pm). Closed Sunday.*

Average Prices: A la Carte £9.50; wine £5.50 per bottle.

Sevens Wine Bar is well known for its lively and friendly atmosphere. A beamed black and white timbered building, it has recently been enlarged to take parties of 50 and modernised at the same time, with air conditioning introduced. Outside in the pretty walled garden is a barbecue for summer lunches.

BUNKERS RESTAURANT at Crondall Golf Course

Heath Lane, Crondall, near Farnham. Tel: (0252) 850880

Hours:	*Open for morning coffee, lunch and dinner (last orders 9.30pm). Closed Sun/Mon evenings.*
Average Prices:	*Business lunch £7.50 (2 courses); dinner £9.95 (2 courses); Trad. Sun lunch £8.95 (3 courses); bar snacks from £3.50.*
Wines:	*House red £6.15 per bottle; white £7.75 per litre.*

Those in search of something different rather than just a place to wine and dine should look no further than Bunkers Restaurant. Under the direction of Chef de Cuisine Terry Adams, food is creative and imaginative with exciting textures and flavours to suit every palate, including the vegetarian. The tastefully furnished, spacious restaurant enjoys panoramic views over the golf course and olde worlde village of Crondall. In the kitchen Terry's culinary style is adventurous, international and light. Unusual starters include light parsley flavoured profiteroles, filled with Roquefort cheese and served on a creamed asparagus sauce, and there are main courses like escalope of veal, flavoured with ginger and coriander, rolled with sautéed kidneys and served with a cognac-flavoured coarse grain mustard sauce. The extensive two-course dinner menu changes monthly, with the exception of favourites like steak Diane, steak au poivre and boeuf Stroganoff which are flambéed at the table. Attractive conference facility.

THE JOLLY FARMER

Guildford Road, Runfold, near Farnham.
Tel: (025 18) 2074

Hours: *Open for coffee, lunch and dinner (last orders*
10pm). Bar meals available.

Average Prices: *A la Carte £10.50; Sun lunch £7; snacks from £1.50.*

Wines: *House wine £7 per carafe.*

The A31 from Guildford to Farnham runs along the Hog's Back, an area of countryside where the North Downs become squeezed together. The Jolly Farmer is a large pub with an air of comfortable prosperity. Deep rich red velvet curtains and carved wooden tables are surrounded by a jumble of bric a brac; old prints, paintings and pottery all add to the effect. The restaurant is situated to the side of the main pub area and provides home-cooked food from fresh local produce. Try Jolly Farmer smokies (smoked haddock with prawns and mushrooms in a cheese sauce) or mussels served on a half shell with a cheese and wine sauce. Desserts include caramel walnut meringue and raspberry Pavlova. At lunchtime there is a hot and cold buffet/carvery, supplemented by various dishes of the day. Sunday is popular for its traditional family roast lunches, with jazz in the evenings. Outside, the garden has a children's play area and barbecues are held, weather permitting, in the summer months.

The
Jolly Farmer
Runfold

TEL: RUNFOLD (025 18) 2074

BENTLEYS

Elstead Mill, Elstead.
Tel: (0252) 703333

Hours: *Open for lunch and dinner. Closed Sat lunch/Sun*
                 evening.
Average Prices: *A la Carte £25; Table d'Hôte lunch £12.50.*
Wines: *House wine £7.50 per bottle.*

Elstead Mill dates back to the Domesday survey when it was one of six listed in the Farnham area. Much of it was destroyed by fire, however, in 1647 when Cromwellian troops used it as a billet. It was largely rebuilt, but the interior has remained much the same ever since, its machinery now on working display and its timber-framed roof looking down upon Bentleys Restaurant. A largely French menu is served with, for example as starters, crêpe de saumon et homard Mornay (a pancake of salmon and lobster with a Mornay sauce) and crevettes Pacifique au Marsala (peeled large prawns, sautéed with garlic, Marsala and cream, served on a bed of rice) and ogen melon Bentleys (half ogen melon filled with strawberries and cherry brandy). There is a good selection of main courses and sweets are from the trolley. The mill is set over a peaceful stretch of the River Wey and surrounded by 15 acres of countryside. It is, therefore, an ideal venue for wedding receptions and other functions and celebrations.

Dine over the River Wey . . . *Bentleys*
ELSTEAD MILL
FRENCH CUISINE
COCKTAIL BAR
. . . in the heart of Surrey

Business table d'hôte and Sunday luncheon £12.50
Wedding parties and special occasions catered for ★ Live music
Reservations (0252) 703333

SQUIRES HOLT RESTAURANT

Hog's Back, Seale. Tel: (0483) 810272

Hours: *Open for lunch and dinner (last orders 9.30pm).*
Closed Sun evening/Mon.

Average Prices: A la Carte £15; lunch £3–£8; wine £7.50 per litre.

Family-run for the last 25 years, Squires Holt has established its reputation through traditional home-cooked food, with the addition of some Continental specialities. There is a full à la carte selection every evening, a roast for Sunday lunch and a choice of hot and cold dishes for weekday lunch. The restaurant overlooks paddocks, lawns and the celebrated scenery from the Hog's Back.

HOG'S BACK (A31),

SEALE, NEAR FARNHAM

Telephone: GUILDFORD 810272

Traditional English and International Cuisine, served in attractive surroundings. A full à la carte menu is available in the restaurant, and there are plenty of bar meals too.

THE WITHIES INN

Compton, near Guildford.
Tel: (048 68) 21158

Hours: *Open for lunch and dinner (last orders 10pm).*
Closed Sun. Bar meals.

Average Prices: *A la Carte £15; Sun lunch £8; snacks from £1.50.*

Wines: *House wine £6.75 per bottle.*

Standing on the edge of Compton Common, near to Loseley Park and the wooded countryside beloved of Victorian artist G. F. Watts, is The Withies Inn. 16th century origins are revealed in low beaming and a traditional atmosphere. Through autumn, winter and spring, steaks grilled over charcoal form the basis of The Withies' reputation. These are complemented by a selection of à la carte dishes such as half roast duckling with an orange or peach sauce, fillet of beef Wellington and chicken Kiev with savoury rice. During the summer months the grills are discontinued and the emphasis changes to fish and an array of salad dishes, imaginatively presented. These include poached halibut with a prawn and brandy sauce, and scampi meunière with mushrooms. When the weather permits meals can be taken outside in the trellised arbour. Real ales are on draught at the bar. The inn lies off the B3000, one mile south of the A3.

For the Best in Traditional English Cuisine
COMPTON, Nr. GUILDFORD
Tel: (048 68) 21158

THE CLAVADEL HOTEL

Epsom Road, Guildford.
Tel: (0483) 69066

Hours: *Open for coffee, lunch, tea and dinner (last orders 9.15pm, 9.50pm Sat). Closed Sun evening.*

Average Prices: *A la Carte £13; Table d'Hôte £10.95; Sun lunch £7.95.*

Wines: *House wine £5.75 per bottle.*

The Clavadel Hotel is a quiet and relaxing hotel set in one of Guildford's quieter corners. Its restaurant aims to marry the enjoyment of good food with wine and the list detailing the latter is both expansive and well-explained. The menu itself is French-based and starts with dishes such as salade tiede (breast of pigeon served on a bed of Continental lettuce and topped with a raspberry vinaigrette), or salade de oie fumé (slices of avocado and smoked breast of goose with a honey mayonnaise). Main courses include selle de chevreuil rôti (saddle of venison with a cranberry and pear sauce), délice de sole royale (fillets of sole filled with salmon mousse and served with a white butter sauce) and poussin poêle estragon (pot roasted baby chicken stuffed with nuts and tarragon and glazed with honey). Sweets are from the trolley and cheeses are supplied by France's Maître Fromager, Androuet. Alternatively, for an extensive, unusual and often changing selection of real ales try The Chase Bar.

THE MANOR AT NEWLANDS

Newlands Corner, Guildford. Tel: (0483) 222624

Hours: *Open for lunch and dinner (last orders 9.30pm).*
            Bar meals.

Average Prices: *A la Carte £20; Table d'Hôte £10.50; Sun lunch £10.50.*

Wines: *House wine £7 per bottle.*

The Manor at Newlands was built at the turn of the century by the London Editor of The Spectator, who believed that it enjoyed the finest view in all Surrey. Today's hotel maintains its period style — its restaurant dominated by a huge chandelier — and overlooks nine acres of gardens and National Trust land in the distance. Andrew Brett is the resident chef who cooks to an English style with French leanings. From the à la carte selection comes smoked salmon and trout roulade, garnished with whipped cream and a prawn dressing, for starter. Salmon also features on the main course, diced with sole and prawns, wrapped in lettuce and poached in sparkling wine. Also available are the popular and filling Manor grills, and dishes such as venison fillet marinated in raspberry vinegar and pepper, sautéd in butter and sweetened with a redcurrant sauce, garnished with apple, mango and kiwi fruit. There is a separate dessert menu with tempting dishes like croque en bouche (pyramid of choux pastry balls, coated in chocolate, filled with crème pâtissière on a light sauce anglaise).

GUILDFORD'S COUNTRY HOUSE HOTEL AND RESTAURANT

The Manor
at Newlands

RAC ***

AA ***

FOR THE FINEST ENGLISH CUISINE
Fully Licensed Bar and Restaurant
Set in 9 acres of parkland · 20 luxuriously appointed bedrooms
reception and conference facilities for up to 150
GUILDFORD (0483) 222624
Newlands Corner, Guildford (3 miles east of Guildford on A25 to Dorking)

(as featured on the outside front cover)

*Enjoy superb cuisine
in the most beautiful
romantic candlelit setting*

**West Clandon · Near Guildford
Telephone: Guildford (0483) 222447**

THE ONSLOW ARMS INN

West Clandon, near Guildford. Tel: (0483) 222447

Hours: *Open for coffee, lunch and dinner. Closed Sun evening/Mon. Bar meals, except Sun evening.*

Average Prices: *A la Carte £19; Table d'Hôte lunch £11.95.*

Wines: *House wine £8.25 per bottle; £6.95 per carafe.*

The village of West Clandon sits at the foot of the Clandon Downs and has long been associated with the Onslow family who lived at Clandon Park, now a National Trust property. Taking their name, The Onslow Arms dates back to 1623, its age revealed through a wealth of old beaming, carved settles and an unusual roasting spit, all contributing to the traditional and warm atmosphere. There is a carvery serving home-cooked food which includes roast ribs of Scotch beef and steak and kidney pie, as well as a separate chilled salad bar. Alternatively, diners have a choice between an extensive à la carte selection and a popular table d'hôte luncheon menu, both created by chef Ewart Morgan. Typical of the selection of dishes may be chicken with mango and steak bordelaise. During the summer months it is pleasant to sit outside in the arboured garden, whilst the chill of the winter months can be seen off in the oak-beamed bar with its gleaming copper, fresh flower arrangements and real ales like Brakspear's, Young's and Courage Directors. The inn also has facilities to handle receptions and other functions.

The Charming Restaurant of the Onslow Arms Inn

POTTERS STEAK HOUSE

Mytchett Place Road, Mytchett, Camberley.
Tel: (0252) 513934

Hours: *Open for coffee, lunch and dinner (last orders 10.45pm, 10.15pm Sun). Bar meals, except Sun.*

Average Prices: *A la Carte £10; bar snacks £1–£4.*

Wines: *House wine £4.90 per bottle.*

Its location is just one of Potters' many attractions. Situated alongside the recently renovated Basingstoke Canal, it enjoys extensive views in peaceful countryside noted for its natural beauty. The Steak House caters for both adults and children. Begin with country pâté with a salad garnish and hot toast, or fresh melon with cherry and orange. To follow there is a full range of steaks with various sauces — chasseur, Diane, au poivre and more, numerous grilled dishes (such as lamb cutlets with mint), fish, poultry and vegetarian dishes. All main course selections are served with French fries or jacket potato, with sour cream or butter. There are some interesting desserts to conclude, with, for example, Pina Colada gâteau and rich chocolate brandy truffle, and speciality coffees like Potters Orange Surprise with Grand Marnier. Captain Bob's Pirate Menu for kids offers such favourites as fish fingers, followed by funny face ice cream. There is also a play area for children and a waterside patio where adults can enjoy a pre-dinner drink.

POTTERS STEAKHOUSE

Mytchett Place Road, Mytchett, Camberley
Tel: Farnborough (0252) 513934

THE LAKESIDE INTERNATIONAL HOTEL

Wharf Road, Frimley Green, near Camberley.
Tel: (0252) 838000

Hours:	*Open for lunch and dinner (last orders 11pm).* *Bar meals.*
Average Prices:	*A la Carte £17; Sun lunch £12.50; business lunch £9.50.*
Wines:	*House wine £6.50 per bottle.*

The Lakeside International Hotel lives up to its name in setting, décor and cuisine. Situated on the edge of a lake, it has the spacious air and modern comforts of a large hotel. The restaurant which overlooks the lake is open-plan with a low ceiling and a contrasting deep red and cream colour scheme. A piano plays soothingly in the background and a choice of seasonal dishes, à la carte, is served. From the list of starters choose from champignons frits à la miel (fried baby mushrooms in batter and rolled in honey) or bisque d'homard (lobster soup with cream and brandy). For a main course there is poached salmon in a hollandaise sauce and piccata de veau cavalieri (slices of veal dipped in egg, topped with Gruyère and surrounded with a tomato concasse, Madeira and red and green noodles), whilst dessert sees pancakes with a lemon, chocolate or cherry preserve as an alternative to the laden sweet trolley. The hotel's facilities lend themselves to a variety of functions; there is even a Mississippi river boat moored to the front of the hotel and available for hire.

FRIMLEY HALL

Portsmouth Road, Camberley.
Tel: (0276) 28321

Hours: *Open for lunch, tea and dinner (last orders 10pm).*
Average Prices: *A la Carte £25; Table d'Hôte £14.75; Sun lunch £13.75.*
Wines: *House wine £6.95 per bottle.*

Enclosed within four acres of wooded lawns and grounds stands Frimley Hall, a late Victorian country house with the recent addition of a glass domed conservatory which blends harmoniously into the period style. The Wellington Restaurant (to which it is attached) offers both à la carte and table d'hôte selections of seasonal English dishes such as Cornish lobster and scallop soup, flavoured with armagnac brandy, or country style terrine of duck and hare with a variety of wood mushrooms, for starters. Main course dishes include fillet of beef forestière (cooked with truffle and wild mushrooms, flamed in brandy with double cream), breast of duckling on a bed of paw paw fruit with a Cointreau and pink grapefruit sauce, or, for vegetarians, individual baked aubergine filled with a variety of beans and savoury vegetables, topped with lattice pastry and served with oriental rice and a tomato sauce. Sweets are from the trolley and there is a selection of cheeses served with apples, celery, nuts and biscuits. The hotel is also well-equipped to cope with the most demanding of board meetings and large business conferences.

FRIMLEY HALL HOTEL

PORTSMOUTH ROAD, CAMBERLEY, SURREY.
Telephone: Camberley (0276) 28321

SULTAN'S PLEASURE

13 London Road, Bagshot-by-pass, Bagshot.
Tel: (0276) 75114

Hours: *Open for dinner 6.30–10.30pm. Closed Sun/Mon.*
Average Prices: *A la Carte £16.50.*
Wines: *House wine £6.80 per bottle.*

Ahmet Ouzoun originally trained in the art of classical French cooking, but since opening a restaurant recalling his native Turkey with his wife, June, he has never looked back. The strains of Turkish music and subdued lighting from original Turkish brass lanterns form a backdrop to a menu that is unusual to English palates. For a starter there is karniyark (garlic flavoured stuffed aubergines), humus salatasi and taramasalatasi (red caviar). For the main course there is a selection of kebabs, şaşliks, T-bones, lamb and fresh chicken, all marinated in wine and herbs and cooked over an open charcoal fire — the traditional Turkish way. Probably the most popular dish on the menu is şaşlik şiş kebab (lamb cut into squares, grilled on the charcoal fire with mushrooms, peppers and onions and served, as with all other main course dishes, with a mixed side salad and brown pilau rice). To round off, try sütlü börek (wafer thin pastry filled with cream custard). Turkish wines and liqueurs make a suitable accompaniment and pleasant finishing touch.

The attractive interior of The Sultan's Pleasure, Bagshot,
where diners can enjoy the delights of Turkish Cuisine.

Food for Thought

Some Sound Advice For That Dining Out Experience

Eating out can be both very enjoyable and very expensive and, in order to get your money's worth, a bit of forethought is well worthwhile; it can make or break what should be an entirely pleasurable occasion.

One of the first things to consider is the top amount you are prepared to spend. Drinks in the bar and at the table can knock your estimate sideways, making your plastic card curl at the edges when the bill is presented. So, armed with money, cheque book and credit card, decide

on the particular type of food you wish to enjoy and the degree of luxury or simplicity you are looking for. Don't lose sight of the fact that, hopefully, you are going to be paying for a meal skilfully cooked

and efficiently served – not footing a bill simply for décor and atmosphere.

Take time to study the menu and don't be rushed into ordering by an impatient member of staff. Decide on a main course first and then match a suitable starter. Remember that it is pointless to go to a restaurant, however beautifully appointed, which specialises in fish dishes only to order steak, or vice versa. A famous chef at one of London's top hotels always made a point of analysing the orders which came into his kitchen; dishes chosen with interest and skill which complemented each other were given particular attention. Rich dish followed by rich dish was treated with contempt – the person ordering was clearly not worth cooking for.

Wine lists can make fascinating reading, yet for many people the selection of wine is embarassing, difficult and confusing. Don't be afraid to talk to the wine waiter and consider his suggestions, but bear in mind what you have ordered from the menu and then decide what you want, not what you think you ought to have. Beaujolais, Chablis, Liebfraumilch and others have become household names, yet lesser known wines are often far more interesting and enjoyable

without being any more expensive. Only by experiencing new tastes can one hope to build up practical knowledge of one of life's great pleasures. Inevitably, a wine may be chosen which is not, perhaps, up to expectation, but this is no excuse for returning the bottle (unless it is clearly bad) – just put it down to experience. And it is worth remembering that salads, often fresh and appetising to look at, if eaten covered with dressing, will turn the wine you are drinking instantly into vinegar.

A little detective work based on a knowledge of seasonal foods will quickly show-up an establishment which depends not on the ability of the chef but on how well the deep-freeze has been stocked and the microwave operated – you might just as well eat at home. However, mass produced, pre-cooked dishes have shown considerable advances in recent years and are often very

hard to detect, particularly when they have been 'improved' by the addition of cream or wine, so the customer can only rely on the integrity of the restaurateur.

Should your meal prove to be disappointing, don't be afraid to mention this to the restaurant manager (assuming that it is a result of poor food or service). When expressed in polite terms, such comments are valued by caterers; after all, their business depends on giving satisfaction. If you are not happy, most restaurateurs would rather you tell them than tell all of your friends!

Finally, don't forget to reserve your table in advance to ensure that you avoid possible disappointment, and, if you can't make the appointment, to always ring with your

cancellation. Plan well, order carefully, keep an eye on the bill and you have the recipe for a very enjoyable experience.

Glossary

To assist readers in making the sometimes confusing choice from the menu, we have listed some of the most popular dishes from restaurants featured in *Where to Eat* up and down the country, together with a brief, general explanation of each item. Of course, this can never be a comprehensive listing — regional trends result in variation in the preparation of each dish, and there's no accounting for the flair and versatility of the chef — but we hope it offers readers a useful guideline to those enigmatic menu items.

STARTERS

Foie gras .... duck or goose liver, often made into pâté
Gazpacho .... a chilled Spanish soup of onion, tomato, pepper and cucumber
Gravad lax .... raw salmon marinated in dill, pepper, salt and sugar
Guacamole .... a creamy paste of avocado flavoured with coriander and garlic
Hummus ..... a tangy paste of crushed chick peas flavoured with garlic and lemon
Meze .... a variety of spiced Greek hors d'oeuvre
Moules marinière .... mussels in a sauce of white wine and onions
Samosa .... small pastry parcels of spiced meat or vegetables
Satay .... small skewers of grilled meat served with a spicy peanut dip
Taramasalata .... a creamy, pink paste of fish roe
Tzatziki .... yoghurt with cucumber and garlic
Vichyssoise .... a thick, creamy leek and potato soup, served cold

FISH

Bouillabaisse .... chunky fish stew from the south of France

Coquilles St Jacques .... scallops
Lobster Newburg .... with cream, stock and, sometimes, sherry
Lobster thermidor .... served in the shell with a cream and mustard
                            sauce, glazed in the oven
Sole Walewska .... a rich dish of poached fish in a Mornay sauce with
                            lobster
Sole bonne femme .... cooked with stock, dry white wine, parsley and
                            butter
Sole véronique .... poached in a wine sauce with grapes
Trout meunière .... floured, fried and topped with butter, parsley and
                            lemon

MAIN COURSES

Beef Stroganoff .... strips of fillet steak sautéed and served in a sauce of
                            wine and cream
Beef Wellington .... beef in a pastry crust
Boeuf Bourguignon .... steak braised in a red wine sauce with onions,
                            bacon and mushrooms
Chateaubriand .... thick slice of very tender fillet steak
Chicken à la King .... pieces of chicken in a creamy sauce
Chicken Kiev .... crumbed breast filled with herb butter, often garlic
Chicken Marengo .... with tomato, white wine and garlic
Chicken Maryland ..... fried and served with bacon, corn fritters and fried
                            banana
Osso buco .... knuckle of veal cooked with white wine, tomato and onion
Pork Normandy .... with cider, cream and calvados
Ris de veau .... calves' sweetbreads
Saltimbocca alla romana .... veal topped with ham, cooked with sage
                            and white wine

Steak au poivre .... steak in a pepper and wine sauce
Steak bordelaise .... steak in a red wine sauce with bone marrow
Steak Diane .... steak in a peppered, creamy sauce
Steak tartare .... raw, minced steak served with egg yolk
Tournedos Rossini ...... fillet steak on a croûton, topped with foie gras and truffles
Wiener Schnitzel .... escalope of veal, breadcrumbed and fried

SAUCES

Aioli .... strong garlic mayonnaise
Anglaise .... thick white sauce of stock mixed with egg yolks, lemon and pepper
Arrabbiata .... tomatoes, garlic and hot peppers
Béarnaise .... thick sauce of egg yolks, vinegar, shallots, white wine and butter
Carbonara .... bacon, egg and Parmesan cheese
Chasseur .... mushrooms, tomatoes, shallots and white wine
Dijonnaise .... cold sauce of eggs and mustard, similar to mayonnaise
Hollandaise .... egg yolks and clarified butter
Mornay .... creamy sauce of milk and egg yolks flavoured with Gruyère cheese
Pesto .... basil, marjoram, parsley, garlic, oil and Parmesan cheese
Pizzaiola .... tomatoes, herbs, garlic and pepper
Provençale .... tomato, garlic, onion and white wine
Reform .... pepper and white wine with boiled egg whites, gherkins and mushrooms
Rémoulade .... mayonnaise with mustard, capers, gherkins and herbs, served cold

DESSERTS

Banoffi pie .... with toffee and banana
Bavarois .... cold custard with whipped cream and, usually, fruit
Crème brûlée .... caramel-topped, rich vanilla flavoured cream
Crêpes Suzette .... pancakes flavoured with orange or tangerine liqueur
Parfait .... chilled dessert with fresh cream
Pavé .... square shaped light sponge
Pavlova .... meringue-based fruit dessert
Sabayon/zabaglione .... whisked egg yolks, wine and sugar
Syllabub .... whipped cream, wine and sherry
Zuccotto .... a dome of liqueur-soaked sponge filled with fruit and cream
Zuppa inglese .... an Italian trifle

CULINARY TERMS

Coulis .... a thin purée of cooked vegetables or fruit
Croustade .... a case of pastry, bread or baked potato which can be filled
Devilled .... seasoned and spicy, often with mustard or cayenne
Dim-sum .... various Chinese savoury pastries and dumplings
Duxelles .... stuffing of chopped mushrooms and shallots
En croûte .... in a pastry or bread case
Farce .... a delicate stuffing
Feuilleté .... filled slice of puff pastry
Florentine .... containing spinach
Goujons .... thin strips of fish
Julienne .... cut into thin slices
Magret .... a cut from the breast of a duck
Mille-feuille .... thin layers of filled puff pastry
Quenelles .... spiced fish or meat balls
Roulade .... stuffed and rolled
Sauté .... to brown in oil
Tournedos .... small slice of thick fillet

Index

ALPHABETICAL INDEX TO ESTABLISHMENTS

i

ALPHABETICAL INDEX TO TOWNS AND VILLAGES

*Peckish
in Perth?*

*Hungry
in Holyhead?*

*Famished
in Felixstowe?*

*Ravenous
in Roscommon?*

WHERE TO EAT

The discerning diner's guide
to restaurants throughout
Britain and Ireland

*Copies available from bookshops
or direct from the publishers*
Kingsclere Publications Ltd
Use the Order Form overleaf

ORDER FORM

To:

KINGSCLERE PUBLICATIONS LTD.
Highfield House, 2 Highfield Avenue, Newbury, Berkshire, RG14 5DS

Please send me

_____ copies of *WHERE TO EAT in BERKSHIRE* @ £1.95 £ _____

_____ copies of *WHERE TO EAT in BRISTOL, BATH & AVON* @ £2.50 £ _____

_____ copies of *WHERE TO EAT in CORNWALL* @ £1.95 £ _____

_____ copies of *WHERE TO EAT in CUMBRIA & THE LAKE DISTRICT* @ £1.95 £ _____

_____ copies of *WHERE TO EAT in DORSET* @ £1.95 £ _____

_____ copies of *WHERE TO EAT in EAST ANGLIA* @ £2.95 £ _____

_____ copies of *WHERE TO EAT in EAST MIDLANDS* @ £1.95 £ _____

_____ copies of *WHERE TO EAT in GLOS & THE COTSWOLDS* @ £1.95 £ _____

_____ copies of *WHERE TO EAT in GUERNSEY* @ £0.80 £ _____

_____ copies of *WHERE TO EAT in HAMPSHIRE* @ £1.95 £ _____

_____ copies of *WHERE TO EAT in HERTS, BUCKS & BEDS* @ £1.95 £ _____

_____ copies of *WHERE TO EAT in IRELAND* @ £1.75 £ _____

_____ copies of *WHERE TO EAT in JERSEY* @ £0.80 £ _____

_____ copies of *WHERE TO EAT in KENT* @ £2.95 £ _____

_____ copies of *WHERE TO EAT in NORTH EAST ENGLAND* @ £1.95 £ _____

_____ copies of *WHERE TO EAT in OXFORD & OXFORDSHIRE* @ £1.95 £ _____

_____ copies of *WHERE TO EAT in SCOTLAND* @ £1.95 £ _____

_____ copies of *WHERE TO EAT in SOMERSET* @ £1.50 £ _____

_____ copies of *WHERE TO EAT in SURREY* @ £1.95 £ _____

_____ copies of *WHERE TO EAT in SUSSEX* @ £2.95 £ _____

_____ copies of *WHERE TO EAT in WALES* @ £2.95 £ _____

_____ copies of *WHERE TO EAT in WILTSHIRE* @ £1.95 £ _____

_____ copies of *WHERE TO EAT in YORKS & HUMBERSIDE* @ £1.95 £ _____

p&p at £0.50 (single copy), £1 (2–5 copies), £2 (6 copies) £ _____

GRAND TOTAL £ _____

Name ....

Address ....

....

Post code .... Cheque enclosed for £ ....

Your help in answering the following would be appreciated:

(1) Did you buy this guide at a SHOP ☐ TOURIST OFFICE ☐ GARAGE ☐ OTHER ☐

(2) Are any of your favourite eating places *not* listed in this guide? If so, could you please supply names and locations ....

....

....